FIFTY YEARS OF UNILEVER

Fifty Years of Unilever

1930–1980

W. J. READER

HEINEMANN : LONDON

William Heinemann Ltd
10 Upper Grosvenor Street, London W1X 9PA

LONDON MELBOURNE TORONTO
JOHANNESBURG AUCKLAND

© Unilever Limited 1980
First Published 1980

ISBN 0 434 62501 9

Designed by Jonathan Sharp
Filmset by Tradespools Ltd, Frome, Somerset
Printed and Bound in Great Britain by
Fakenham Press Ltd, Fakenham, Norfolk

*Frontispiece: The Wealth Machine—Original cartoon by
Heath: Drawn for* Unilever Magazine

*Below and facing page: Early advertising for a margarine
called Palmin in Germany about 1910.*

Contents

	Foreword	vii
	A Note on Sources	ix
	Acknowledgements	xi
Chapter 1	The Founding Fathers	1
Chapter 2	Unilever in the Thirties	19
Chapter 3	Interval for Catastrophe	41
Chapter 4	Transformations	55
Chapter 5	Multinational Life and Times	91
Chapter 6	Unilever at Fifty	115
	Index	145

Foreword

This book is more of a co-operative undertaking than most. The text is mine and I take full responsibility for it, but I should like to thank Judy Slinn for her research and for her work, together with Richard Wilson and Maureen Staniforth, on the pictures. They have been immensely helped by many individuals, unknown to me, in Unilever companies throughout the world.

Tony Fisher and Michael Cullen in London, Hans Heinrich, Arie Braakman and Jan van Ommen in Rotterdam have helped and encouraged me throughout, and I should also like to thank the two Secretaries, of Unilever Limited and Unilever NV, for finding time to read the text so carefully and to comment on it so constructively.

In preparing the typescript, no one could have been more helpful than Daphne Middleton.

Charles Wilson's *History of Unilever*, a pioneer in its field, is indispensable to anyone seeking to understand the development of the company, and I am deeply indebted both to the book and to its author.

March 1980   W. J. R.

Opposite: Mr W. H. Lever bought this advertisement on a visit to the USA where it had already proved most effective. Lightening the burden of housework has been an important ingredient in the success of Lever Bros and subsequently of Unilever.

A Note on Sources

Over the last fifty years a great deal has been written about Unilever, some of it friendly, some of it hostile, some of it, like the Report and Accounts, simply informative. A short list, chiefly of the more recent publications, follows:

UNILEVER PUBLICATIONS

Chairmen's Speeches, 1930–1979
Lord Heyworth and Paul Rijkens began a tradition of speeches ranging over wider topics than the affairs of Unilever. The tradition has continued under their successors, though generally with rather closer application to Unilever, and among recent speeches are the following:

Lord Cole and H. S. A. Hartog, 1967: Private Enterprise and the Profit Motive.

Sir Ernest Woodroofe and G. D. A. Klijnstra, 1973: Unilever in Today's Society.

Sir Ernest Woodroofe and G. D. A. Klijnstra, 1974: Countering Inflation—the Unilever Contribution.

Sir David Orr and H. F. van den Hoven, 1977: Unilever and European Integration.

Sir David Orr and H. F. van den Hoven, 1978: Unilever and the Third World Food Problem.

Sir David Orr and H. F. van den Hoven, 1979: Unilever Management in a Changing World.

Other Unilever Publications
Sir Ernest Woodroofe: The Social Role of Multinational Enterprises, 1973.

Sir Ernest Woodroofe: Unilever and World Development, 1973.

H. F. van den Hoven: The International Company and Developing Countries, 1975.

O. Strugstad: Practical Advantages to Developing Countries from the Transfer of Technology, 1977.

H. F. van den Hoven and H. Meij: Information Document for the International Symposium on Eurofinance, 1979.

W. J. Reader: Hard Roads and Highways—SPD 1918–1968, 1969.

W. J. Reader: Birds Eye—The Early Years, 1963.

OFFICIAL PUBLICATIONS

United Kingdom Government:
Reports of the Monopolies Commission on: Household Detergents, 1966.

Proposed Merger of Unilever and Allied Breweries, 1969.

Frozen Foodstuffs, 1976.

United Nations:
Multinational Corporations in World Development, 1973.

The Impact of Multinational Corporations on Development and on International Relations, 1974.

GENERAL PUBLICATIONS

Sir Michael Clapham: Multinational Enterprises and Nation States—Stamp Lecture, London, 1975.

Counter-Information Services: Anti-Report on Unilever, 1975.

David Fieldhouse: Unilever Overseas, 1978.

Andrew Knox: Coming Clean, 1976.

Wally Olins: The Corporate Personality, 1978.

The Politics and Health Group: Food and Profit, 1979.

Graham Turner: Business in Britain, 1969.

Charles Wilson: The History of Unilever, 2 vols, 1954.

Charles Wilson: Unilever 1945–1965, 1968.

Acknowledgements

We acknowledge with gratitude permission to reproduce the following:

Page 17: 'The Unilever Galaxy' reprinted from The Economist, UK, 27th December, 1930.

Pages 27 and 52: Cartoons from Story of Margarine by S. F. Riepma, President of the National Association of Margarine Manufacturers, USA.

Page 89: Information on chart reprinted from the Fortune world business directory—1979 Time Inc.

Our grateful thanks also go to Unilever companies throughout the world who have supplied photographs of which only a small selection has been able to be reproduced in this book.

I.

The Founding Fathers

On Monday September 2nd 1929 the decision was taken which brought Unilever into being on January 1st 1930. For about a year negotiations had been going on between two small groups from the United Kingdom and the Netherlands who represented on the one hand the Margarine *UNI*on and on the other hand *LEVER* Brothers Limited.*

Those two names were blankets. They covered two groups of businesses brought into being over a period considerably longer than the 50 years we now celebrate, extending over every continent, active in shipping, African merchandise, meat, cattle food, ice cream and much else as well as the margarine and soap with which most people in 1929 identified them.

The negotiators had not set out to amalgamate the two groups but to keep them apart. They were both very large users of oils and fats for whom the world's sources of supply were scarcely large enough, and each had expanded into the other's activities, Levers having taken to making margarine, the other side soap, while both were oil-millers, and the situation was uncomfortable. Why not disentangle?

After about six months, late in 1928 and in the spring of 1929, the negotiators realised that they could not simply pull the groups to bits and then remould them nearer to their hearts' desire. Could they, perhaps, group all the soap businesses under Levers, all the margarine under Margarine Union, and form a joint 'middle company' for edible fats and milling? They found they could not, and the whole negotiation was in some danger of breaking down, but it did not. Attraction

---

* The name Unilever seems to have been coined immediately the decision to merge was taken. The name of the coiner has undeservedly been lost.

Opposite: Margarine was only invented in 1870. To make progress against butter it was advertised heavily. This poster was used in Germany in the early 1900's.

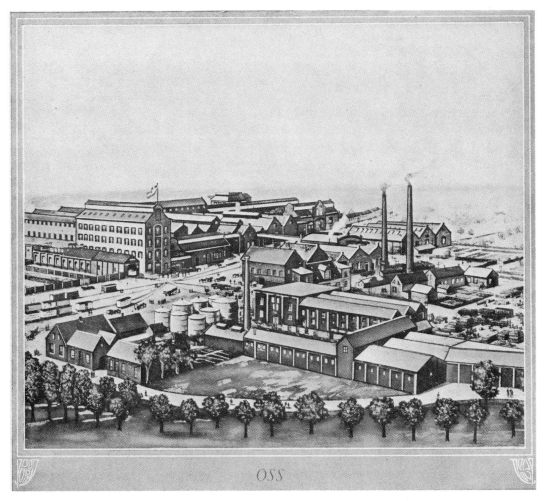

OSS

proved stronger than repulsion, total merger was agreed upon, and Unilever was the result.

The strongest bond of union between the two groups, though not at first the most obvious, was their common reliance on the same final customer: the housewife. They had both prospered on rising standards of working-class living in late 19th century Europe: Dutch margarine makers first, Levers somewhat later.

Van den Berghs and Jurgens, rival firms of Dutch butter merchants, became rival manufacturers of margarine in the 1870's. They found their markets in the large industrial towns of Great Britain and the booming German Empire.

W. H. Lever, later Lord Leverhulme (1851–1925), shrewdly switching from grocery into soap in the mid-'80's when raw material prices were low, and having found a first-class new

Anton Jurgens United (Margarine) Works at Oss, where the Jurgens family had started as butter merchants.

product—Sunlight Soap—launched his brand on to the English working-class market with all the force of modern marketing methods behind it, building goodwill which no retailer could ignore. By the end of the century he had one of the largest soap businesses in the world.

These were the nuclei around which the merging groups of 1929 had formed. By 1929 the Margarine Union consisted of Van den Berghs, Jurgens, the large Central European firm of Schicht, Hartogs' meat business at Oss, and other members. It was strong and prosperous, firmly rooted on the Continent and in

Opposite: Lever's mill at Port Sunlight produced oil for soap and margarine making and turned the residues into cattle food.

2

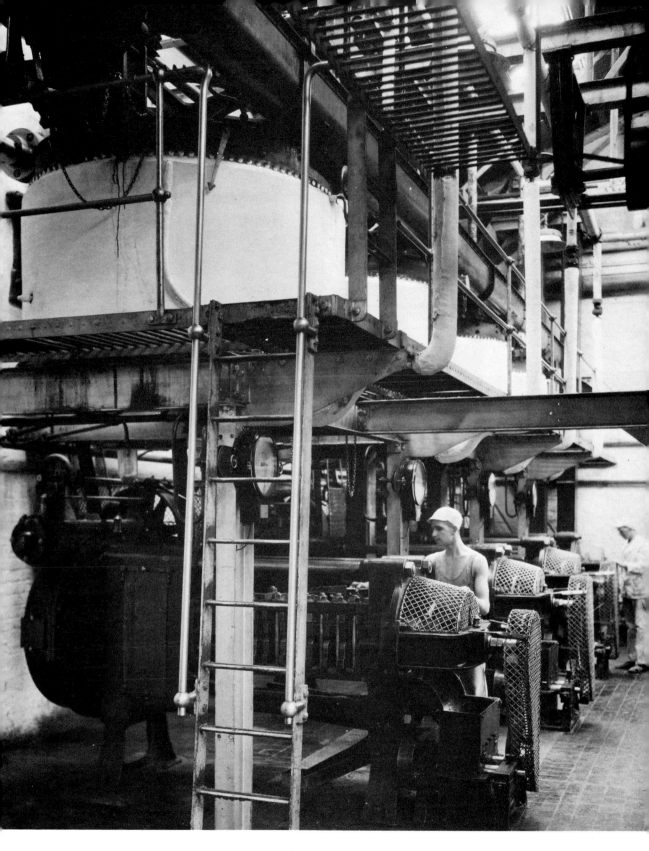

The children all know me!

I'm the WALL'S ICE CREAM MAN

I stop at all homes where the Wall's Ice Cream "W" card is displayed in the window.

STOP ME & BUY ONE

T. WALL & SONS LTD LONDON & GODLEY

33

WALL'S ICE CREAM

PURE RICH CREAM
FRESH FRUIT JUICES
SOUND FOOD VALUE

SNOFRUTES 1ᵈ
LARGE BRICKS 1'6
SMALL BRICKS 9ᵈ
CHOC. BARS 4ᵈ
TUBS 4ᵈ
BRICKETTES 2ᵈ

I will deliver to your home any of the five different kinds of delicious and healthful Wall's Ice Cream.

Here they are:

Wall's Ice Cream Bricks—9d.

(double size 1/6)

Wall's Ice Cream Brickettes —2d

Wall's Ice Cream Tubs—4d

Wall's Chocolate Coated Ice Cream Bars—4d

Wall's Snofrute (pure fruit juices, Pasteurized and frozen in moulds)—1d

Wall's Ice Cream is food—wholesome, appetising, nourishing food.

Good to eat—
Good for you—

The purity and high quality of Wall's Ice Cream is attested by the Institute of Hygiene

WALL'S TUBS

WALL'S SNOFRUTE

Try Wall's Ice Cream in your home to-day

WALL'S ICE CREAM

—brought to your door daily

W

Over 1,500 tricycles are used in the distribution of Wall's Ice Cream.

ICE 2A-208

Above: Thames Paper Co (renamed Thames Board Mills) was one of Lord Leverhulme's acquisitions in the early 1920's.

Opposite: Wall's developed ice cream in the 20's and 'Stop me and buy one' became a national institution.

the United Kingdom, without major interests in the wider world, although explorations had been made.

Lever Brothers, under the propulsive power of the founder's genius, latterly erratic, had ramified far more widely and variously. In response to the raw material problem Lever had established himself in plantations and African trading; in competition with the Dutch makers he had gone into margarine; to disembarrass himself of private interests which he no longer required he had sold to Lever Brothers Mac-Fisheries, Angus Watson, Pelling Stanley, Wall's and other businesses which later pro-

vided the foundation for a large part of Unilever's business in food products but of which the blessings, at the time of sale, were somewhat heavily disguised.

Levers' geographical range was much wider than the Margarine Union's. They had interests on the Continent, but the heart of Lever Brothers' business, as with most British businesses of the day, was in the United Kingdom and the British Empire, meaning chiefly, for soap, the countries then known as the Dominions and India. Levers' largest subsidiary, very much so, was the United Africa Company, formed in 1929 by merging the Niger Company, Leverhulme's largest and most rashly undertaken acquisition, with its rival the African & Eastern Trade Corporation. UAC were West African merchants, with their main trading base in Nigeria.

Of the two partners to the merger of 1929, the Margarine Union was the stronger, offering considerable attractions to the Lever Board who had been passing through an anxious period of reconstruction, from 1921 onward and especially after Leverhulme's death in 1925, during which it had been necessary to make good the consequences of the Niger Company purchase and other ill-advised ventures.

On the other hand, to the Margarine Union, Levers' wide geographical span was extremely attractive, for they were beginning to find European markets cramping. Moreover the reconstruction of Levers under Francis D'Arcy Cooper (1882–1941), whom they respected, was going well and there was no need to doubt the Lever group's underlying soundness. There was a very solid platform of common interest and complementary advantage. The founders of Unilever built on it.

Unilever was the product of a very large merger indeed, comparable with the merger three years earlier which had produced Imperial Chemical Industries, up to that time the largest merger carried out in Great Britain, or with the formation of IG Farben Industrie in Germany in 1925. Unilever was also international in a way in which ICI and the IG were not, for the parent companies of the two merging groups were English and Dutch, so that a form of organisation was required which would give due weight both to the Dutch and English partners and avoid the risk of double taxation,

Above: Sir Francis D'Arcy Cooper, Chairman of Unilever Limited 1930–1941.

Below: Trucks laden with copra outside the head office of the Philippine Refining Co in about 1930.

Opposite: William Hesketh Lever, first Lord Leverhulme 1851–1925.

Far left: Samuel van den Bergh, 1864–1941.

Centre left: Anton Jurgens, 1867–1945.

Left: Paul Rijkens, the successor, in 1933, to Anton Jurgens as effective head of Unilever NV.

Below: A Pelling Stanley truck with an advertisement for R. D. Hume products—one of the predecessors of today's John West Foods.

in the United Kingdom and the Netherlands, under the law as it stood at the time.

This was a problem which Van den Berghs had faced in one of their earlier merger operations. They had worked out an answer which they presented to the Margarine Union in 1927 and which the Margarine Union presented to Unilever in 1929. At the head of the new groups two holding companies were set up, one English, capitalised in sterling, based in London—Unilever Limited; the other Dutch, capitalised in guilders, based in Rotterdam—Unilever NV. The two companies had identical Boards and an Equalisation Agreement between them provided that they should at all times pay dividends of equivalent value in sterling and in guilders. NV, broadly speaking, looked after Unilever's interests in continental Europe; Limited those in the United Kingdom and 'overseas'.

The merger agreement, dual in form, had unity for its paramount object, and as soon as it came into force in 1930 the architects of the merger were faced with the hardest part of their task: to overcome the mutual antipathy felt by rivals of half-a-century thrust suddenly into each other's arms; to dispel the feelings of uneasiness which mergers always create, often

justifiably, within the merging businesses; in short, to make the new whole greater than the sum of the old parts. This was especially the conception of the professional managers, and the idea may have come to their minds more easily than to the minds of members of the founding families who had been owners of the businesses battling against each other. It was above all the idea of Francis D'Arcy Cooper of Levers and of Paul Rijkens of Van den Berghs.

There should be no question, they were determined, of playing off the interests of soap against the interests of margarine; the interests of one family against another; the interests of 'the English side' against the interests of 'the Dutch side'. The only question now ought to be 'What is the interest of Unilever?'

Left: A Lever salesman visiting a Birmingham shop in the 1960's as, no doubt, his predecessors had at the turn of the century. (The name Persil is only used by Unilever in the UK and France—elsewhere in Europe it belongs to Henkel.)

Opposite: One of the many margarine brands owned by Unilever after the 1930 merger—Rama in Germany.

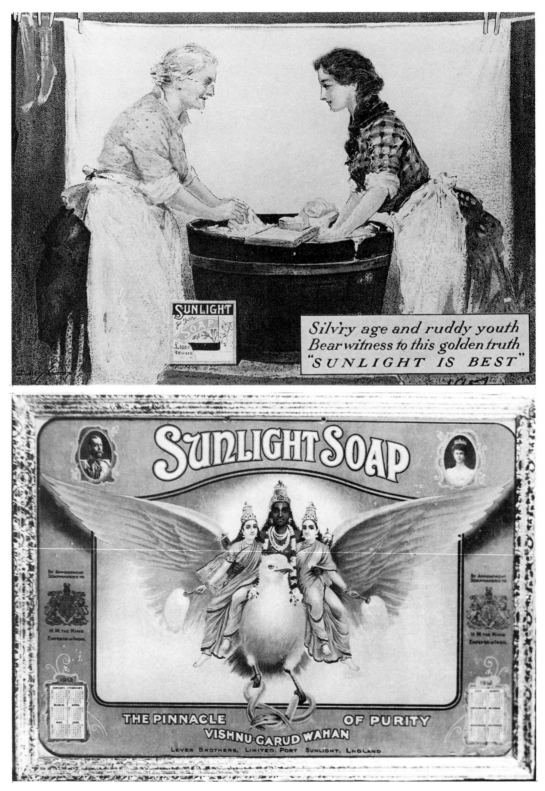

*Opposite, top: 1911 advertisement for Sunlight Soap painted
by Dudley Hardy who, with John Hassall, was one of the
pioneers in the revival of the artistic poster in the 1890's.
Hardy had established a European reputation as a painter.*

Opposite, below: India—a tin plate calendar, 1912.

Above: Lever's Italian factory at Valtorta in the 20's.

Right: Kenya, 1928.

Opposite: The opening of Unilever NV's new Rotterdam Head Office in 1931—Blueband, Sunlight and Radion girls.

Above: The Schicht business was an important part of the 1930 merger and it was especially strong in Eastern Europe.

Below: Early advertising for margarine did not hesitate to compare itself with butter.

THE UNILEVER GALAXY.

OF the outstanding business combinations of recent years, the building up of the Unilever combine has been one of the most noteworthy. The fusion of the Margarine Union group and Lever Brothers in December, 1929, the securing of control of United Africa, and the subsequent acquisition of a majority interest in a group of provision stores in Great Britain, constituted one of the biggest industrial amalgamations in European history. There was brought under single dictation, as far as trading policy and finance were concerned, a group of companies of world-wide ramifications and multitudinous functions, extending from the production of vegetable oils in the tropics to the catching of whales in the Antarctic, from the manufacture and marketing of margarine, soap, perfumeries, and cattle foods to the retailing of groceries and the keeping of fish shops and restaurants.

This colossal combination began with the amalgamation in 1927 of two old-established margarine manufacturing companies—Anton Jurgens and Van den Berghs—which had subsidiaries operating in most European countries. Margarine Unie was formed to take over the Continental companies of both groups, and Margarine Union, Limited, to acquire the English companies. The reason for this dual organisation was the avoidance of double taxation. In 1929 Margarine Unie extended its interests widely in German, Danish and other European companies engaged in the margarine trade. It came to an agreement with the Schicht and Hartog concerns, both manufacturers of margarine and soap, which was of great importance to its control of the European trade. Finally, in September, 1929, it amalgamated with Lever Brothers. This involved the fusion of the numerous Lever subsidiaries with those of the Margarine Union group, and the changing of the name Margarine Union to Unilever. One of the subsidiaries of the Lever group was the Niger Company, which had already merged (in April) with the African and Eastern,

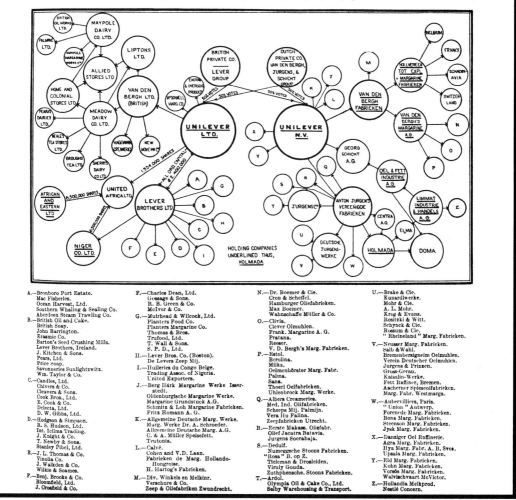

A.—Bronboro Port Estate.
Mac Fisheries.
Ocean Harvest, Ltd.
Southern Whaling & Sealing Co.
Anderson Steam Trawling Co.
B.—British Oil and Cake.
British Soap.
John Barrington.
Erasmic Co.
Barton's Seed Crushing Mills.
Lever Brothers, Ireland.
J. Kitchen & Sons.
Pears, Ltd.
Price Soap.
Savonneries Lightzwitz.
Wm. Taylor & Co.
C.—Candles, Ltd.
Chivers & Co.
Cleavers & Sons.
Cook Bros., Ltd.
E. Cook & Co.
Delecta, Ltd.
D. W. Gibbs, Ltd.
D.—Hodgson & Simpson.
R. S. Hudson, Ltd.
Int. Icilma Trading.
J. Knight & Co.
T. Newby & Co.
Stanley Pibel, Ltd.
E.—J. L. Thomas & Co.
Vinolia Co.
J. Walkden & Co.
Wilkie & Soames.
F.—Benj. Brooke & Co.
Bloomfield, Ltd.
J. Crosfield & Co.

F.—Charles Dean, Ltd.
Gessage & Sons.
R. B. Green & Co.
G.—Mulrhead & Wilcock, Ltd.
Planters Food Co.
Planters Margarine Co.
Thomas & Bros.
Trufood, Ltd.
T. Wall & Sons.
S. P. D., Ltd.
H.—Lever Bros. Co. (Boston).
De Levers Zeep Mij.
I.—Huileries du Congo Belge.
Trading Assoc. of Nigeria.
United Exporters.
J.—Berg Märk Margarine Werke Isser-stedt.
Oldenburgische Margarine Werke.
Margarine Grundstuck A.G.
Schmitz & Loh Margarine Fabricken.
Fritz Homann A.G.
K.—Allgemeine Deutsche Marg. Werke.
Marg. Werke Dr. A. Schroeder.
Allgemeine Deutsche Marg. A.G.
C. & A. Müller Speisefett.
Teutonia.
L.—Calvé.
Cohen and V.D. Laan.
Fabricken de Marg. Hollando-Hongroise.
H. Hartog's Fabricken.
M.—Div. Winkels en Melkinr.
Verschure & Co.
Zeep & Oliefabricken Zwundrecht.

N.—Dr. Boemer & Cie.
Cron & Scheffel.
Hamburger Oliefabricken.
Max Boemer.
Wahnschaffe Müller & Co.
O.—Clivia.
Clever Olmuhlen.
Frank. Margarine A. G.
Pratana.
Reoer.
V. D. Bergh's Marg. Fabricken.
P.—Estol.
Berolina.
Milka.
Oelmcohörster Marg. Fabr.
Palma.
Sana.
Thoerl Oelfabricken.
Q.—Albers Creameries.
Med. Ind. Olifabricken.
Scheeps Mij. Palmijn.
Vera Ilu Falina.
Zeepfabricken Utrecht.
R.—Eerste Makaas. Oliefabr.
Olief Jacutra Batavia.
Jurgens Socrabaja.
S.—Deduif.
Numegsche Stoonz Fabricken.
"Rosa" B. op Z.
Ticleman & Drosleiden.
Viruly Gouda.
Zuthphensche. Stoonz Fabricken.
T.—Ardol.
Olympia Oil & Cake Co., Ltd.
Selby Warehousing & Transport.

U.—Brake & Cie.
Kunardlwerke.
Mohr & Cie.
Max Boemer.
A. L. Mohr.
Krog & Evans.
Rositzki & Witt.
Schynck & Cie.
Rossum & Cie.
"Rheineland" Marg. Fabricken.
V.—Neuser Marg. Fabricken.
Salb & Wahl.
Bremenbensigneim Oelmuhlen.
Verein Deutscher Oelmuhlen.
Jurgens & Prinzen.
Gross-Gerau.
Kaisalin-Werke.
Fett Rafliner, Bremen.
Aacherner Spiesscolfabricken.
Marg. Fabr. Westmarga.
W.—Aubervilliers, Paris.
" Union " Antwerp.
Forenede Marg. Fabricken.
Bona Marg. Fabricken.
Steenson Marg. Fabricken.
Jysk Marg. Fabricken.
X.—Danziger Oel Raffinerie.
Agra Marg. Fabricken.
Ilya Marg. Fabr. A. B. Svea.
Upsala Marg. Fabricken.
Y.—Eld Marg. Fabricken.
Kohn Marg. Fabricken.
Vorsås Marg. Fabricken.
Walvischvaart McVictor.
Z.—Hollandia Melkprod.
Nestlé Concern.

Opposite, top: A witty fishmonger (spot the pun) in Bridgwater, England, in the 30's.

Above: The Unilever Galaxy, as depicted in The Economist, United Kingdom, 27th December 1930.

Opposite, below: Niger House, Lagos—1929.

2.
Unilever in the Thirties

No years in this century, perhaps in any century, have a worse reputation than the 1930's, worse even than the reputation of the bloodstained '40's, for in some countries, for some people, they can be invested with a certain heroic glamour which the '30's lack. The '30's began with economic disaster and ended with world war. Unemployment rates rose to 25 per cent or more in the United States, Germany and the Netherlands: in the United Kingdom, briefly, almost to 20 per cent. Farmers and primary producers, alike in North America and in the poorest parts of Africa and South America, suffered from a chronic failure of demand. From the chaos in Germany Hitler arose. Under his impact Europe crashed into a disaster greater even than that of 1914, the full effects of which have not yet worked themselves out.

The '30's passed almost immediately from reality into folklore, and folklore never loses anything in the telling. Gloom, nevertheless, was not quite so unrelieved and universal as folk memory suggests. Whilst economic recovery in the United States was painfully slow and the Nazis throve in Germany, the United Kingdom, one of Unilever's most important markets, recovered rapidly from the worst of the slump. Outside the depressed areas, real wages rose and the standard of living improved.

Nevertheless in the early days of Unilever, after the collapse of prices on the New York Stock Exchange late in October 1929 set wider disasters in train, the outlook before the makers of Unilever was not encouraging, for there seemed to be no side of the business that did not stand to suffer from the world economic crisis. In so far as it was a crisis of primary production it affected margarine by throwing

Opposite: Truly a period piece—the Thirties.

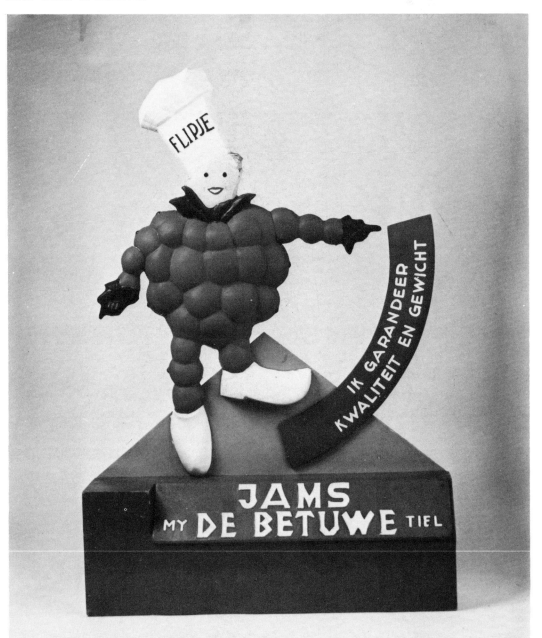

cheap butter on the market, oil-milling by reducing the demand for animal feeds, and raw materials by disastrous and unpredictable falls in the prices of oils and fats. In so far as it was a crisis of industry it affected the market for nearly all the goods except animal feeds which came out of Unilever factories because they were intended for working-class households whose livelihood might disappear.

Above: De Betuwe (Netherlands) shop display 1938.

Opposite: Angus Watson products 1939—Design for 10 ft poster—'Skippers, Delicious!' by Graham Simmons.

Above: Consumer products in the 30's—Thames Board packaging; they manufactured for other customers as well as Unilever, and still do.

Opposite: Advertisements for margarine in the 30's stressed its butter-like qualities.

In this atmosphere the administrative organisation of the new business was set up, largely by drawing on the experience of the constituent partners. The dual framework was taken over from Van den Berghs. From Levers the founders took the design for their central executive body: the Special Committee, set up in London in September 1930. This was and still is a committee of the Board exercising very wide powers so that operations throughout the world could be directed with unquestionable authority. The Special Committee's essence was that it was small, and capable of quick, unanimous action.

At first it had eight members, later no more than three, a number found by experience to be large enough to comprehend a wide range of talent but not so large as to weigh down the springs of action.

Under the authority of the Board, channelled through the Special Committee, control was partly geographical, partly functional. To look after Unilever companies on the Continent of Europe, a Continental Committee was set up. To look after companies elsewhere, except for the United Africa Company and companies in the United Kingdom, Unilever took over another Lever administrative device: the Over-

seas Committee, which was reasonable since most of the overseas companies came from the Lever side. In the United Kingdom, where operations were much larger and more varied than elsewhere, there were three executive bodies: the Home Soap Executive, the Margarine Executive, the Oils and Fats Executive. To serve the whole business, everywhere and in all its aspects, advisory and service departments were set up in London and Rotterdam.

From the underlying principle of unity and from this system of organisation it followed that the managers of the business should be offered careers open to talent, unimpeded by considerations of family, nationality, or former company

Unilever NV's Head Office, Museumpark, Rotterdam, was completed in 1931 (photograph 1955).

associations. The idea did not make instant, universal appeal, but Anton Jurgens pushed it home. The merger agreement provided that the Lever group should appoint one-half of the members of the holding-company Boards and the Jurgens, Van den Bergh and Schicht groups the other half. Just before Anton retired, he proposed that vacancies should be filled according to ability irrespective of other considerations. His proposal was accepted and a decisive step was taken towards the multinational Board of the late 1970's. By 1937 the profits of Unilever Limited were about twice as great as the profits of Unilever NV, largely as a result of circumstances—in particular, the policies of the German Government—which neither company could control,

and it seemed desirable to redistribute the assets in the interests of greater equality. Nearly all the ex-Lever assets outside the British Empire, including the large and prosperous American business, were sold to NV.

Such a measure would have been inconceivable only eight years before, at the time of the merger. Even in 1937 it took all Cooper's persuasiveness and authority to carry it through. Nevertheless it was done, showing how thoroughly the ill-will of over half a century had been dissipated and how the energies which had formerly served the parts were being devoted to the well-being of the whole. For the merger to be justified, Unilever had to be able to carry out drastic and unpopular measures and survive. It passed the test triumphantly. Not all merger companies do.

A still more disagreeable and contentious task

had to be taken in hand before the full benefits of the merger could be expected to show: the rationalisation of production and marketing. Where so many competitors had come together, overlapping and duplication were inevitable, especially in factories, in sales forces, in the number of brands on the market.

The problem had been recognised and tackled by Margarine Unie on the Continent between 1927 and 1929, but when Unilever came into being it found itself with ten factories for mar-

garine and edible fat in the British Isles. By 1937 production had been concentrated in two major and three minor plants. The rest had been closed. Manufacturing costs had beer halved: freight costs cut by a third.

On the soap side of the business in the United Kingdom there were in 1931 49 manufacturing companies with 48 sales organisations, selling hundreds of product lines. This luxuriant forest was drastically thinned out during the '30's, largely on the basis of proposals by Geoffrey Heyworth, later Chairman of Unilever Ltd. Marketing effort was concentrated on far fewer brands, designed to cover—but no more than cover—the various uses of household washing products, produced in a few large manufactur-

ing centres and sold by fewer representatives. There were to be no more than two or three Unilever brands, perhaps half a dozen at the

Unilever House, London. Unilever Ltd's Head Office was completed and opened in 1932.

Rulers from West Africa visit Unilever House, Blackfriars, 1934. Col Beddington (centre), Chairman of UAC, has the Sultan of Sokoto on his left and the Emir of Gwandu on his right. (The other European is the interpreter.)

outside, in any field of use, instead of hundreds getting in each other's way, but the surviving companies were encouraged to compete with each other.

On the Continent, too, the number of factories, of brands, of salesmen were all cut down. In the end Unilever faced its rivals, especially the ubiquitous German firm of Henkel, with an organisation for making and selling soap which was simpler, less costly and more efficient than the collection of ex-rivals which it had inherited from the merging companies.

The largest task of rationalisation was in Africa, for the United Africa Company, itself the product of a very large merger, faced the consequences of one of the fundamental elements in the world crisis: the slump in primary produce. The UAC's capital was written down by half in 1931. Its management at home and in Africa was reduced. The whole basis of its trading activities was reviewed and, as a con-

sequence, more attention was paid to lines of business outside the traditional limits of the West African trade, and therefore less severely hurt by the collapse of the market in primary produce.

While these painful measures were in hand, the margarine business was governed by the deplorable state of farming throughout the world. Butter stood at absurdly low prices, especially in the United Kingdom, and nearly all governments except the British took drastic action to protect their own butter from the competition of margarine. In Germany, as soon as the Nazis came to power, the economic motive for protecting the farmer was reinforced by considerations of strategy. They had learnt the lesson of 1914–18 when Germany had been cut off from supplies of margarine-makers' raw materials.

All over the Continent and in the USA (not then an important market for margarine) Unilever, in common with other makers, found itself harassed by all manner of devices for protecting butter. Discriminatory taxes, excise duties, restrictions on production, compulsory mixing of butter with margarine—all these measures and more were put into force in one country or another during the 1930's.

Margarine sales, nevertheless, were very nearly back by 1938 to their level in 1929, before

Right: Comment on the struggle between margarine and butter (USA).

(Batchelor in the New York Daily News)

Below: Van den Berghs exhibition at Milan, 1930.

Methods of manufacturing margarine have developed a great deal since the 30's.

The picture far left shows margarine being packed at Purfleet in the 1930's so that it may be compared with automatic packing at Van den Bergh en Jurgens' factory in Rotterdam in 1966 (near left).

The cutout below shows margarine being made at Van den Berghs' Purfleet factory in the UK in the 1930's.

Pages 30 and 31: Advertising for Lux Toilet Soap—'Nine out of Ten film stars use Lux' was created in the United States and developed so that it became one of the great world-wide campaigns. The selection of advertisements on the following two pages shows how it developed with changing tastes and styles.

Top, left to right: 1930, 1933, 1942. Bottom, left to right: 1946, 1949, 1958 and early 60's.

the slump. Rationalisation was partly responsible: so also was an improved product and a determined effort to raise the standing of margarine in the public mind by advertising. Trade was urged more and more towards high-grade brands reinforced with vitamins, such as Stork in the United Kingdom and Blue Band in the Netherlands.

Experienced men in the soap trade in the later '20's were inclined to think, in D'Arcy Cooper's words, that it had reached 'a fixed state'. They were wrong. The '30's saw both change and—in spite of the depression—expansion. For many years, with a rising standard of living, demand had been swinging from hard soap towards flakes and powders. In the '30's it swung faster. Rising expectations also encouraged the launch of soapless detergents which were to take over so much trade from soap in the 30 years to come. Those were the changes. The expansion came particularly in toilet soaps,

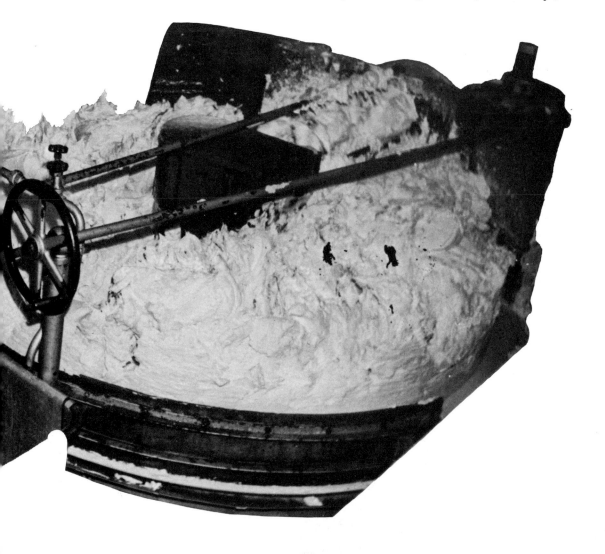

another product associated with high standards of living, and toilet-soap marketing in the United States, the United Kingdom and many other countries in the '30's ('Nine out of ten film stars use *Lux* . . .' etc) bore out the claim often made for good advertising on a large scale that it can help to make goods cheap enough for far more people to afford them.

Unilever, relying a great deal on the experience of Lever Brothers Company in the USA (which few Americans thought of as European-owned), developed the new ideas in washing products there, in the United Kingdom, and on the Continent. It was not left to do so in peace.

Procter & Gamble, larger than Lever Brothers in the United States, invaded the United Kingdom in 1930, when they bought the old-established business of Thomas Hedley in Newcastle. They challenged Unilever products, one by one, with all the force of American marketing methods. By the time war broke out they were very formidable. On the Continent there was Henkel's widespread business and in every country there were local competitors.

During the '30's the trade in washing products tended to expand in the more advanced countries and contract elsewhere. In the advanced countries soap was regarded as a necessity and did not cost much in proportion to the total household budget. Over and above that, where real wages rose housewives readily responded to the advertisers, pressing the claims of more and better products. In more primitive countries soap might still be more or less of an 'optional extra' and its price a fairly serious charge on small, falling incomes.

Above: Sunlight Soap was one of a handful of products upon which Unilever companies were built overseas. The picture shows it being packed in Argentina in 1939.

Opposite: An early Sunlight Soap advertisement, 1887.

Pages 34 and 35: In 1930 an advertising campaign began for Persil ('Persil washes whiter') which has been carefully developed ever since and is still highly successful. In the UK Persil is today, as it has long been, the housewife's favourite washing powder. (The name Persil is only used by Unilever in the UK and France—elsewhere in Europe it belongs to Henkel.)

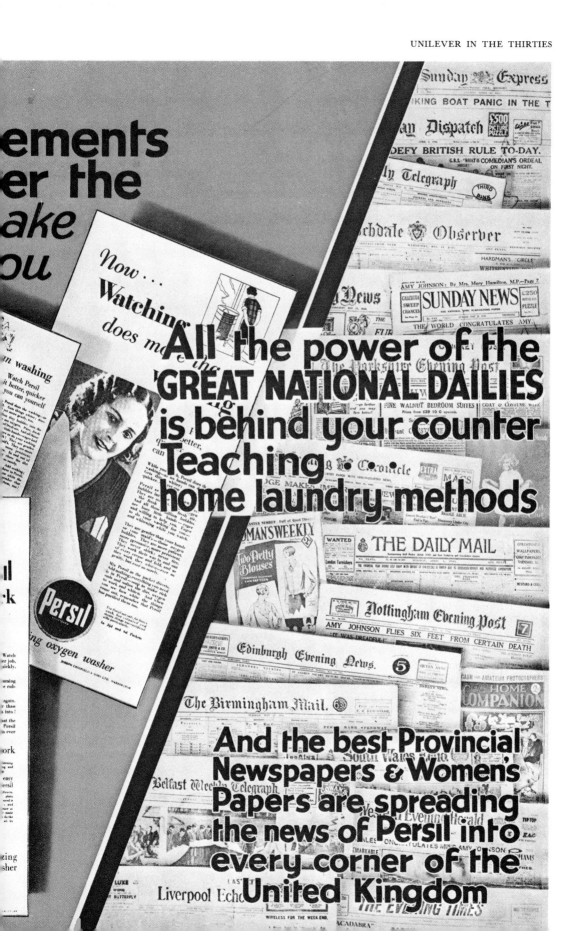

Unilever's sales of washing products throughout the world flattened off and even dropped a little during the worst years of the depression, between 1930 and 1934. Then they rose sharply and in 1939 they were running above 900,000 tons a year: 200,000 tons more than in 1929.

One fortunate by-product of the farming depression, from Unilever's point of view, was a shortage of lard in the United States. It enabled the business to build up, first in the USA and then in the United Kingdom, a flourishing trade in cooking fat made from oil seeds: a trade both valuable in itself and helpful to the oil-millers, especially after 1935.

In the '30's it was fair to look upon Unilever as above all else a business in oils and fats. UAC and the plantations bought or grew oil seeds. The oil-mills processed them (buying, of course, from many other sources of supply, as UAC and the plantations sold to other users). The margarine factories and the soap factories, each in their different ways, worked up oils and fats into finished products and marketed them. The 'margarine side' and the 'soap side' thought of themselves as the most important parts of the business, roughly co-equal, and even in the oil-mills or in West Africa it would have been difficult to quarrel seriously with that view.

There was already another sizeable side to Unilever in Hartogs' meat business in the Netherlands and in the group of businesses which had been Lord Leverhulme's private collection and which, after judicious pruning, were beginning by 1939 to look quite promising. Moreover in 1938 an American called Robert Ducas turned up in England with the rights to a process of deep freezing associated with the name of Clarence Birdseye, and offered them speculatively to Unilever. Convenience foods at that time, however, were scarcely a major part of Unilever's business, certainly nothing to rival margarine and soap, and few were prepared to back them for future expansion. Nevertheless their flags were flying and Geoffrey Heyworth, at least, had noticed which way the wind blew.

Above: Lux being packed in New Zealand in the 1930's.

Opposite: A 1930 Dutch poster for Lux soap flakes.

36

Above: Lifebuoy Advertisement Department cart, about 1900.

Right: Well-known Unilever products had already been widely established in Germany by 1930.

Opposite: Advertisement for Pears Soap, 1917.

37

Above: Demonstrations always played an important role in getting housewives to use brands of margarine. This demonstration was given at Alkmaar, Netherlands, in the 1930's.

Opposite: A French advertisement of the 1930's for brands of margarine.

Waschpulver

für
Weiß- Grob-
Buntwäsche

Inhalt reicht für 2½–3 Eimer
= 25–30 Liter Wasser

Waschanleitungen
beachten!

Gründliches Einweichen und
sorgfältiges Weichmachen
(Enthärten) des Wassers ist
besonders wichtig; genaue
Anweisung siehe Rückseite!

Deutsche Frau, Wäsche ist wertvolles Volksgut!
5. Alle Einweich-, Entfärbungs- und Waschmittel genau
nach Gebrauchsanweisung verwenden. Diese Mittel müs-
sen gut aufgelöst und verrührt werden. Einweichwasser
schadet jeder Wäsche.

Richtiges Waschen hilft sie erhalten!
6. Stark beschmutzte Wäsche besonders
gründlich — evtl. zweimal — einweichen.
7. Uebermäßiges Reiben, Bürsten, Wringen
aus der Wäsche entfernen.

3.
Interval for
Catastrophe

The Second World War, long foreseeable and long foreseen, took about ten years to break out. The Japanese attack on China in September 1931 and the sinking of the American fleet at Pearl Harbour in December 1941 were the first and last links in a chain of events, including those running from Hitler's assumption of power in January 1933 to his assault on the Low Countries and France in May 1940, which carried the world from apparently assured peace to a condition of general war. This rising storm of violence, intricately interwoven with the economic troubles of the times, swept the nations from depression at the beginning of the '30's to an even more desperate predicament at their end.

Unilever, having large interests in Central Europe and in Germany, was embroiled almost from its foundation in the consequences of Government policies framed either for economic self-sufficiency or for war—or, in the case of Germany after 1934, for both. Policies of this kind struck at one of the major assumptions on which international businesses had previously been able to rely: that however much governments might impede the flow of goods across frontiers by tariffs, they would not interfere with the flow of funds by exchange control. Dr Schacht, President of the Reichsbank from 1933 to 1939 and Minister of the Economy from 1934 to 1937, showed how unsound that assumption was. Today, like other assumptions of 19th-century liberalism, it looks pathetically naïve.

The impact of German economic policy on Unilever was spectacular and bizarre. Even before Hitler came to power, the German government had been interfering with the margarine business for the benefit of German farmers and with the transfer of funds for the benefit of the German balance of payments. In

Opposite: Wartime brought austerity. The marketing of brands was often suspended and products became anonymous, like this wartime pack of washing powder from Austria.

well-balanced
SOAP RATION!

PERSIL

No. 1 SOAP POWDER CLASS

For extra whiteness

3½ᴰ packet (6 oz.) 1 COUPON
7d packet (12 oz.) 2 coupons

BODYGUARD

THE SOAP TO BEAT THOSE GERMS

For extra health service

2ᴰ tablet (4 oz.) 1 COUPON

EVE Toilet Soap

For extra complexion care

3ᴰ tablet (3 oz.) 1 COUPON

PURITAN

THE HOUSEHOLD SOAP

For extra lather

2½ᴰ tablet (8 oz.) 2 COUPONS

JC 102-837   All weights shown above are net weight when manufactured

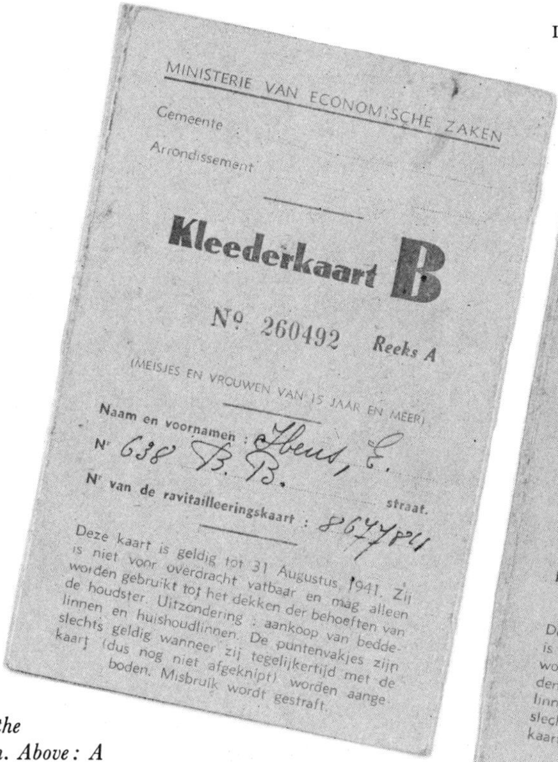

MINISTERIE VAN ECONOMISCHE ZAKEN

Gemeente

Arrondissement

Kleederkaart B

No 260492   Reeks A

(MEISJES EN VROUWEN VAN 15 JAAR EN MEER)

Naam en voornamen : Ibens, E.

No 638 B. B.   straat.

No van de ravitailleeringskaart : 867781

Deze kaart is geldig tot 31 Augustus 1941. Zij is niet voor overdracht vatbaar en mag alleen worden gebruikt tot het dekken der behoeften van de houdster. Uitzondering : aankoop van bedde- linnen en huishoudlinnen. De puntenvakjes zijn slechts geldig wanneer zij tegelijkertijd met de kaart (dus nog niet afgeknipt) worden aange- boden. Misbruik wordt gestraft.

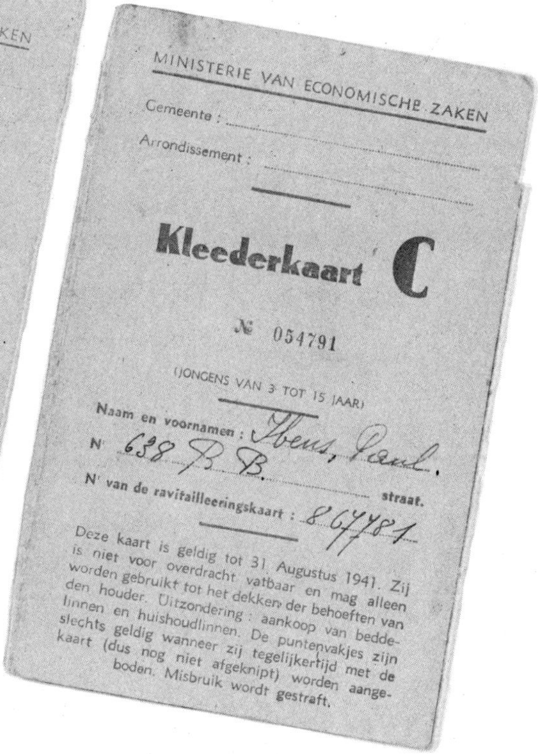

MINISTERIE VAN ECONOMISCHE ZAKEN

Gemeente :

Arrondissement :

Kleederkaart C

No 054791

(JONGENS VAN 3 TOT 15 JAAR)

Naam en voornamen : Ibens, Paul.

No 638 B. B.   straat.

No van de ravitailleeringskaart : 867781

Deze kaart is geldig tot 31 Augustus 1941. Zij is niet voor overdracht vatbaar en mag alleen worden gebruikt tot het dekken der behoeften van den houder. Uitzondering : aankoop van bedde- linnen en huishoudlinnen. De puntenvakjes zijn slechts geldig wanneer zij tegelijkertijd met de kaart (dus nog niet afgeknipt) worden aange- boden. Misbruik wordt gestraft.

Wartime austerity— opposite: this UK advertisement tried to show you how to get the best out of your ration. Above: A Belgian ration book, kindly lent by Mr H. Ibens. Below: Unilever provided an emergency washing service in London during the blitz— an example of this was in Stepney in 1944.

LIFEBUOY

EMERGENCY BATH SERVICE

FREE
HOT SHOWER BATHS
TOWELS AND SOAP
HOT WATER

Czechoslovakia, Austria and elsewhere similar measures were taken for similar reasons. Schacht, serving Hitler and Goering for the benefit of German military power, carried matters further, thereby permanently influencing the structure of Unilever's German business.

This was because German profits, prevented from leaving Germany, had to be invested there far beyond the normal needs of the business. Loans for public utilities absorbed a proportion. Beyond that, Unilever put money into cheese, fish, hair dye, ice cream, a shipping company on the Elbe and other enterprises which, for a business still heavily concentrated on oils and fats, seemed then to make less sense than they might have done later. One legal means of getting money out of Germany arose from another unlikely direction: shipbuilding. Between 1933 and 1939 Unilever financed the building of some hundreds of thousands of tons of varied shipping, and the sale of ships abroad provided a way of transferring funds.

In Europe and in Asia, as the German and Japanese conquerors advanced, the unity of Unilever was shattered. Rotterdam passed under German control and London was cut off from the lost empire in the East. Moreover in neutral countries, if the German government could make a good claim that Unilever NV was the rightful owner, it was necessary to conduct businesses very circumspectly.

The advance of Russian armies deep into Central Europe brought another separation, more lasting—indeed final—and in its wider implications more serious. The means by which communist governments including, after 1947, that of China took over business varied on a scale from purchase to uncompensated seizure. The result was everywhere the same: Unilever from once-promising markets quite shut out. Large areas of Central Europe, the homeland of Schicht, became inaccessible; so did East Germany, Poland and the Baltic states. The losses were heavy for Unilever and for Europe the omens were threatening.

The British wartime government, in which Conservative influence was strong, set up the very model of a socialist controlled economy, single-mindedly devoted to one end: victory. It

Left: War is a stimulant to invention. Fuel shortage in Brazil led Irmaos Lever to seek alternatives. Gazogene was one of them.

Below: In the years before the Second World War in Germany, Unilever acquired a fishing fleet.

Pages 46 and 47: Up to 1948 Unilever had a substantial business in China. Main photograph shows the China Soap Co factory. Inset: The Shanghai Oil Mills.

worked, at the expense of all freedom of choice for the consumer and all possibility of normal development for any business. In Britain and other war-stricken countries sales of Unilever's traditional products—soap and edible fats—held up remarkably well, but brand names disappeared behind the drab covers of the ration book and almost all advance towards new products came to a halt.

LEVER BROTHERS & UNILEVER LTD/NV
ANNUAL SALES OF SOAPS AND EDIBLE FATS
TO THIRD PARTIES (IN METRIC TONS)

Year	Soaps	Edible Fats
1939	913,033	536,642
1940	802,708	571,927
1941	863,566	560,587
1942	801,136	496,163
1943	783,321	512,297
1944	862,887	516,243
1945	860,024	614,651
1946	750,169	559,529
1947	810,638	606,125
1948	940,689	767,311
1949	1,053,586	980,505

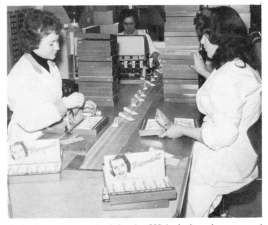

Pepsodent was acquired in the USA during the war and production followed in many other countries soon after. The picture above shows Pepsodent being packed in Finland in 1959.

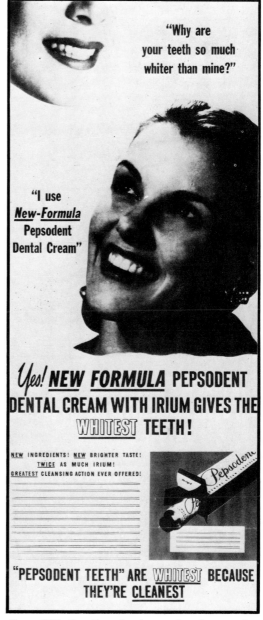

Above: Pepsodent being loaded in Zaire in the 70's.

Left: This lorry was operated by SPD in the UK in 1947.

Above: This Canadian advertisement dates from 1946.

Pages 50 and 51: Unilever factories suffered from destruction during the war. This is what happened to the Vlaardingen plant in the Netherlands.

In the United States, matters were otherwise. There, non-soapy detergents had been emerging as a commercial proposition in the late '30's, and Procter & Gamble were able to go on developing them, leaving Unilever with a very awkward post-war gap to fill. Unilever, for its part, bought the Pepsodent business in 1944 and with it came Charles Luckman. Both were considered very desirable acquisitions. In the United Kingdom the business made a start, but only a start, towards expansion in foods by the purchase, in 1943, of the Birds Eye deep-freezing rights and of Batchelors' canning business—on the strict understanding that there would be no development of either while the war lasted.

The enforced separation of the head offices of Unilever from each other and from the businesses which they had been established to control shattered the organisation built up in the first years after the merger. It put an end also to the centralised system of management by which Unilever had been run in the '30's—you could hardly go to the bathroom, a North American manager with experience of those days is said to have observed, without asking head office first—and to which it might have been expected to return.

It did not do so. Force of circumstances broke the centralising tradition: deliberate decisions of policy made sure that it was not renewed, and these decisions owed a great deal to the personal force of two men at the head of Unilever's affairs in the years immediately after the war: Paul Rijkens and Geoffrey Heyworth. Both were professional managers of long service—Rijkens joined Van den Berghs in 1910, Heyworth, Levers in 1912—without ties of ownership or family interest in any branch of Unilever. Each saw the business as a whole and in its international setting, with a European base and opportunities and responsibilities world-wide. Both, being men of liberal outlook, were averse to dictatorship from the centre and determined to develop the self-reliance of Unilever managements: a determination which some, in the difficult days just after the war, found disconcerting.

The main Board kept control of major capital expenditure and of the appointment, pay and dismissal of senior executives. Otherwise it became axiomatic that as a general rule initiative should lie with the men on the spot. Local

A World War II cartoon by Shoemaker

Above: The butter versus margarine argument continues. Comment from the USA.

Opposite: Joe Scarborough, probably the highest paid 'naïve' artist in England, painted this picture from memory. Joe worked for Batchelors in the laboratory for a couple of years, and with the exception of the Rolls Royce—belonging to the then Chairman, Maurice Batchelor—and the green overalls worn by the women, this outside scene at end of shift hasn't changed a great deal.

managements would be expected to frame their own plans and convince the centre of their rightness. Then, within wide limits, they would be at liberty to pursue their own interests according to local circumstances, local knowledge and their own specialised business experience.

The immediate outlook in 1945 was bleak. Germany, Europe's power-house and one of Unilever's most important markets, was shattered industrially and geographically divided. The Netherlands had suffered heavily from the German occupation and the fighting which got rid of it, and elsewhere in Western Europe there were varying degrees of devastation, far more widespread than after the previous war. Recovery from 1947 onwards was greatly helped by the United States through 'Marshall Aid'.

Above: Lifebuoy 'did its bit' for the Canadian forces. War-time programme cover.

Opposite, above: Sierra Leone—traditional transport. Below: Refrigerated transport on a large scale. SPD containers for Birds Eye, 1974.

The United Kingdom, comparatively lightly damaged both physically and by loss of life, was suffering from economic ailments of long standing, accentuated and complicated by the effects of war, made embarrassingly visible by a chronic deficit in the balance of payments. The USA was aboundingly prosperous and overflowing with confidence in the American way of life, exported with zest in all directions, but the USA was not an easy field for Unilever. From Unilever's point of view one of the brightest spots on the horizon seemed to be in tropical Africa, apparently politically stable and much more prosperous than before the war because of continuing demand for African produce. Nevertheless there was a widespread view among economists, whose advice was taken very seriously, that there was grave danger that the second world war, like the first, would be followed, perhaps after a short unhealthy boom, by widespread depression.

4.
Transformations

Far from collapsing into depression after 1945, the major capitalist economies of the world put right the damage of war with astonishing speed and then launched into a boom which lasted, with comparatively minor fluctuations, for the greater part of the following 30 years. Between 1948 and 1963 industrial production in the countries of the OECD more than doubled: then between 1963 and 1970 increased by nearly 50 per cent again.

Not only were far more goods and services turned out, but many of an entirely new kind, whether nylon tights or voyages to the moon, for nothing, it seemed, could hinder the flow of new technology and the increase in the means of production that went with it. Economic growth had evidently become a law of nature, especially with oil so cheap and adaptable to so many purposes. To promote growth became the chief aim of statesmen, or at any rate of politicians, and to doubt its beneficence became a kind of heresy.

The marvels of the age were the recovery of West Germany and the prosperity of the European Economic Community after the signing of the Treaty of Rome in 1957: in the East, the rise of Japan and one or two much smaller communities (Hong Kong, Singapore) where an injection of Western capitalism into an oriental bloodstream had produced peculiarly potent, highly idiosyncratic results. Great Britain, on the other hand, continued on a path of apparently unstoppable decline: in the '60's, with remarkable insouciance.

Even in Great Britain there was growth, if rather slower than elsewhere, and the boom generally was very profitable for Unilever and for other companies in consumer goods, for the new wealth that was being created flowed very rapidly

Opposite: Chairmen of Unilever NV and Unilever Ltd. Left, top to bottom: F. J. Tempel. 1956–1966. H. S. A. Hartog, 1966–1971. G. D. A. Klijnstra, 1971–1975. Right, top to bottom: Lord Heyworth, 1941–1960. Lord Cole, 1960–1970. Sir Ernest Woodroofe, 1970–1974.

Above: In the UK rationing did not end until 1954. This picture was taken on the day brands came back for margarine and cooking fats.

Opposite: The introduction of Good Luck Margarine in the USA in 1950 was planned to coincide with the repeal of Federal Tax on margarine.

through society in the advanced countries, generating an appetite for goods and services on a scale never known or even dreamt of before and incomes to satisfy it. The consumers' world began to glitter with exciting things: motor cars, television sets, transistor radios or, nearer Unilever's field, refrigerators, freezers, washing machines (needing specialised powders) and a constantly expanding range of 'convenience foods'—all within the means of ordinary families, especially if they were boosted by wives' earnings, instead of being the perquisite of the well-to-do.

The tide of affluence washed outwards, albeit attenuated, towards Africa and Asia. Transistor radios were heard in remote villages. Outboard motors appeared on the stern of dugout canoes. Detergent foam began to float away from dhobi ghats. Heinekens' beer found a market in Nigeria. The style of living of the West, or what it was imagined to be, was held up for admiration and, however improbable, was powerfully attractive. Ancient and primitive societies began to shake themselves to pieces in the struggle to attain it.

At the same time other, more serious, strains were setting in. The drive towards independence from colonial powers became a headlong rush. Population began to rise unmanageably, partly as a result of medical progress, and in many places the struggle for bare subsistence contrasted bitterly with the plenty of the industrial societies and made a mockery of the flow of consumer goods they offered. From the point of view of the poorer nations, the world order

began to look remarkably like the Marxist picture of society in the rising industrial nations of the 19th century, with a privileged class of a few rich countries living off the labour and natural resources of the rest.

All this social turbulence, matched in the industrial countries by rising disenchantment, particularly amongst the young, surged through a world in which the pre-war balance of power had been overthrown. The total and unexpectedly rapid collapse of British power removed the main guarantee of stability over regions stretching from Singapore to the Middle East in one direction and throughout the length of Africa in another. The whole scene was dominated, as it still is, by mutually hostile alliances centred on the USSR on the one hand and the USA on the other, with China an uncertain quantity in between, and with the young, mostly poor, successor states to colonial empires presenting a tempting field for adventures in power politics.

In Unilever's business it has been the richer nations of the world—chiefly, up to now, those in Western Europe and North America—which have set the trend of product development, and over the last 30 or so of Unilever's 50 years the trend has increasingly been for suppliers of consumer goods to sell service as well as substance. Service of course costs money, but the rich have always been willing to pay for it, and the newly affluent consumers of the post-war world have the same instincts as the rich of an earlier day. The more affluent consumers are, the greater the element of service they are prepared to buy, and there have never been such affluent consumers, or so many of them, as during the last 30 years.

In the principle of selling goods that make work easier there is nothing new. 'Why does a Woman look old sooner than a Man?' asked William Lever's advertising about 90 years ago,

Van den Bergh's margarine factory in Nigeria 1954.

58

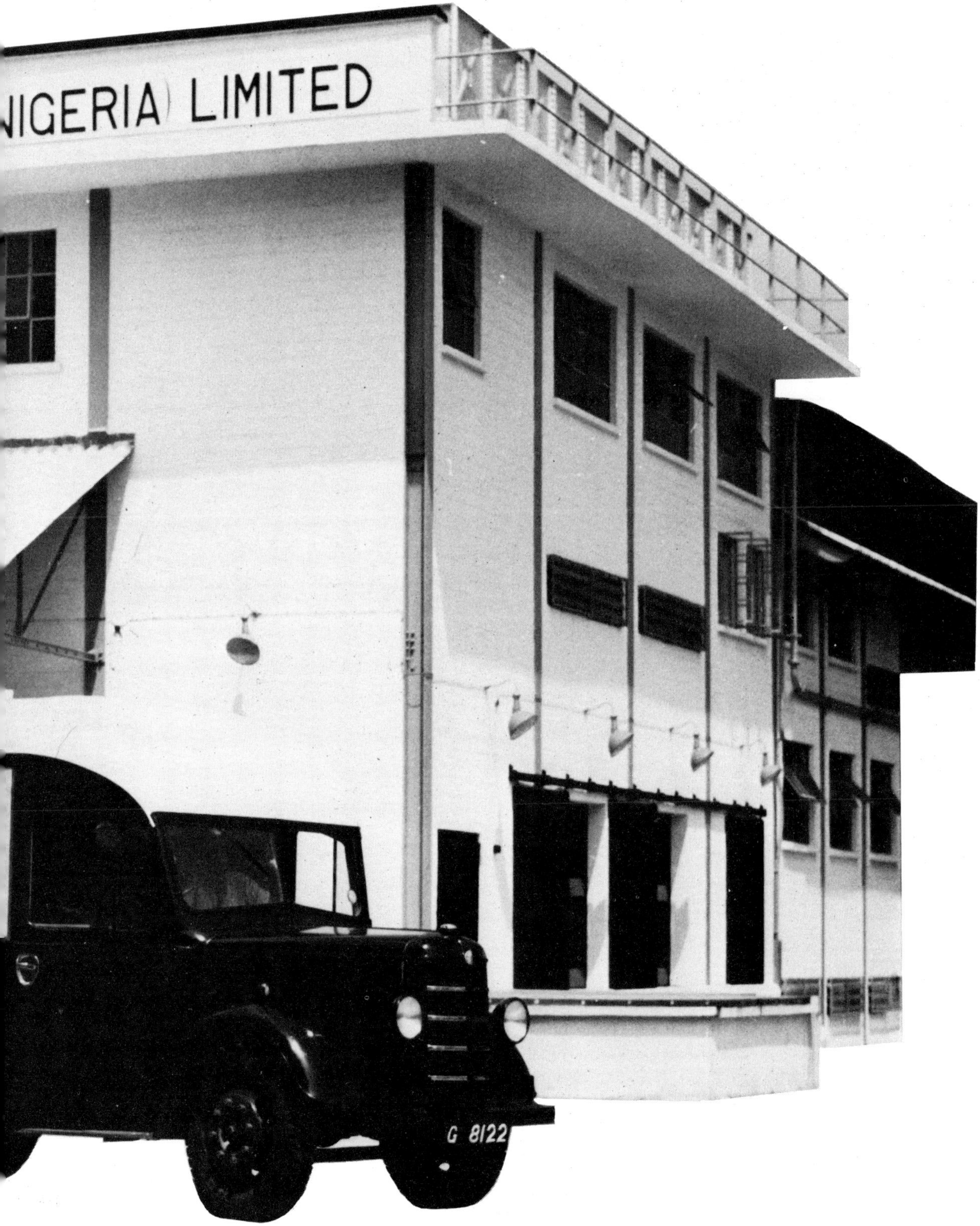
NIGERIA) LIMITED
G 8122

Opposite: Boxes go on forever!—Ceylon.

and gave the answer—because household washing is such hard work. She should use Sunlight Soap which makes it so much easier. That particular tradition has been continued down to the present day, through soap powders, soap flakes and non-soapy detergents to powders specially formulated for washing machines, themselves labour-saving, thereby drastically altering the nature of Unilever's business in washing products by swinging it away from reliance on soap and, through soap, on natural oils and fats towards materials synthesised from petrochemicals. Sales of non-soapy detergents were very small indeed in 1950. By 1965, at about 1½m metric tons, they represented 56 per cent of all Unilever detergents sold.

The move which was to broaden Unilever's range of interests more than any other in its first 50 years, and in time to carry it decisively away from overwhelming dependence on oils and fats and their derivatives, was made on the side of the business dealing with meat products, fish, ice cream and canned goods, which in 1946 provided about 9 per cent of the value of Unilever's turnover. That was a little over half the value of turnover in margarine, edible fats and salad oils, which itself was about a quarter of the value of turnover in oils and fats and products derived from them:

Unilever Total Turnover 1946* of which:		100 per cent
Oils and fats and derivatives:		
Oils and fats	28	
Soap and other detergents	17	
Margarine, edible oils, salad oils	16	
Animal feeds	5	
	—	66
Foods other than margarine etc		9
Other products:		
Merchandise (mainly UAC)	11	
Produce, mainly tropical, including timber	8	
Toilet Preparations	3	
Miscellaneous goods and services	3	
	—	25

* Turnover = Sales to third parties + internal sales, which included much of the turnover in oils and fats.

Above: In many countries film shows, including advertising films, are important ways for promoting brands in areas where mass media do not reach. This example comes from South Africa, 1971.

Right: It is vital to Unilever companies all over the world that products are available wherever there are people—a shop in India.

In the food industries generally the principle of 'convenience'—doing in the factory work which the housewife would otherwise have to do, if she could, in her own kitchen—has a history running well back into the 19th century, linked almost invariably with some form of preservation: factory jam and sauces in glass; biscuits, meat, fish, fruit in metal boxes of various kinds; dried provisions, and so on. There was a good deal of prejudice, at one time justified, against food not prepared at home and against cooks who used it, but standards in the food industries had been rising long before the war and in the United Kingdom and elsewhere tinned salmon and tinned fruit had acquired an aura of mild luxury—very suitable for Sunday tea when the family entertained in state—and perhaps the war did something for canned food, too. Anything as scarce as that had to be desirable.

Over the past 35 years Unilever's business in

convenience foods, already large, varied and geographically widespread, has been greatly expanded. Companies already owned by Unilever have grown. More companies in more countries have been taken over. Technology has been modernised and the range of products has been increased and improved, largely by means of Unilever's own research and development. Dehydration, one of the oldest of all methods of food preservation, which has the advantage that it needs no cold storage, has been developed in various ways so that it can be applied to soups, vegetables and complete meals, thus rescuing Batchelors' business in the United Kingdom from decline and providing food products very suitable for countries where refrigeration, in the home and elsewhere, is less widespread than in Europe and North America.

On this side of the business, as soon as the war was over, Unilever launched into the most ambitious development in a new product field of its first 50 years: frozen foods. It was a project bristling with difficulties. It involved persuading large numbers of farmers to change

Promotions and launches play an important part in keeping a brand lively and growing.

Above: A promotion in Nigeria in 1967.

Cutout centre: The launch of Omo in Argentina in 1962.

Opposite, top: Omo introduced in Rotterdam, Netherlands, 1952.

Opposite, below: Weary counters faced with all the entries for the Omo Dream House Competition in the Netherlands, 1953.

their cropping habits; large numbers of retailers to install cold cabinets; large numbers of housewives to change their buying habits; large numbers of people—most difficult, perhaps, of all—to change their eating habits: four tasks, each daunting enough in itself, which all had to be

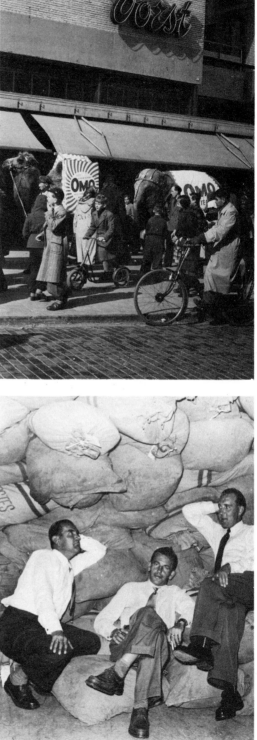

pressed forward at the same time if frozen foods were to succeed. Moreover Unilever had no experience of the frozen food business. It was unknown territory, largely unexplored by anyone outside North America.

Even more than most of Unilever's activities, frozen food needed the backing of immense resources in money, men and patience. It could not be put on the market without a large investment, sustainable over several years without return. Processing plant had to be provided and a specialised distribution system, with cold stores and refrigerated transport. The risks turned out to be very high: higher, surely, than had originally been foreseen. It was intended from the start to develop the business internationally, but development did not go smoothly.

By the late '70's the total market for frozen foods in the United Kingdom was running at more than £700m a year. Birds Eye, which created the market, needed seven or eight years to get firmly established and was more than once in danger of extinction. That actually happened to the businesses in the Netherlands, Belgium and Germany, where early experience drove Unilever out of frozen foods by 1950.

They bought a way back in, expensively, eight or nine years later. There were similar discouragements and episodes of in-and-out-and-in-again elsewhere. All this is worth bearing in mind by anyone tempted to assume, while eating fish fingers, frozen chips and peas in front of a television commercial, that large businesses can thrust unwanted products on the consumer by the effortless exercise of market power.

It is easy and fashionable to be suspicious and scornful of modern factory-produced foods. People say they are not 'natural' (a difficult word to define). They are elaborately packaged. They are heavily advertised. They are rather expensive. The food a cook sends to table she ought to have prepared herself from raw ingredients. Food grown by modern agricultural methods with the aid of artificial fertilisers and pesticides is ecologically damaging and probably dangerous to eat.

Frozen, dehydrated or tinned produce, it may readily be admitted, is not the equivalent of produce fresh-gathered. Dishes prepared in the factory are not the equivalent of dishes prepared by conventional methods by a good cook. Factory foods do, however, represent good value for money, taking account, as many users

A circus in Chile helps to promote Rinso.

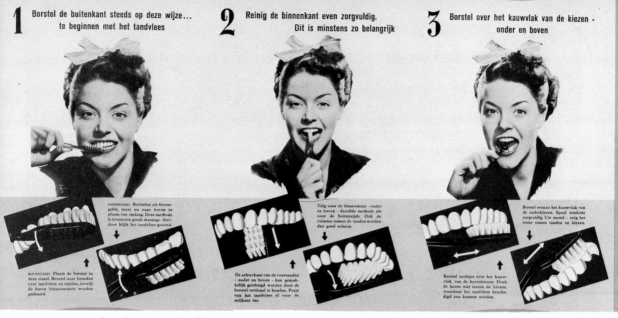

seem prepared to do, not only of the ingredients but of the time and labour which they save both in shopping and in preparation. What is more important is the cheapening of some products and the saving of waste of others which modern methods, serving a mass market, have made possible.

Research directed to breeding chickens for quick growth and high conversion of food to flesh has brought poultry down, in 20 years or so, from a luxury dish to the cheapest form of meat. Pigs, similarly, have been bred to convert food efficiently into meat and to provide a carcass of which very little need be wasted. The food required for these purposes, naturally, is of the highest importance, and a great deal of development work has been done on the animal feeding stuffs side of Unilever, aiming all the time at specific foods for specific purposes in specific animals and poultry.

Before fish could be frozen and processed at sea a good deal of the catch would spoil until it was only fit for fish meal. Today, partly as a result of pioneering work in Unilever, fish can be frozen and filleted as it is caught, fish oil can

Above: Unilever has always believed in education. This chart was prepared for use in schools in the Netherlands.

Right: Even the Town Hall tower comes in useful! Denmark.

Opposite, top: Tinned salmon, a luxury food in the immediate post-war world as, indeed, it is today.

Opposite, below: Birds Eye Foods started up soon after the war and their peas have always been important—a pack of peas in use soon after the war (right) and today's pack.

Above: Dried soups have been successfully marketed by Unilever in many countries. These examples come from Sweden.

Right: Soft, high quality margarines have been an important Unilever development—Doriana is sold in Brazil.

be extracted, fish meal prepared from the offal. At harvest-time, there used to be enormous waste of fruit and vegetables. Quick-freezing, canning, dehydration by large-scale modern methods, allied with mechanical harvesting, have helped to cut it out. They have taken the seasons out of eating, too, if you like it that way.

Battery-rearing of animals is not pleasant to contemplate. Some modern farming practices may be a recipe for disaster. The flavour of mass-produced food products is not to everybody's taste. Nevertheless anyone who condemns them and the practices behind them

Unilever has a meat business in a number of countries. Above: Meat being packed at Hartog's factory, Oss, Netherlands.

Left: Wall's Meat in the UK has paid considerable attention to the development of the best sort of pig for processing.

Opposite: Scado installation producing chemicals in Germany.

should reflect that, but for the modern food industries, there would be nothing like enough food to support people in the advanced countries in anything like the style they have become accustomed to during Unilever's 50 years. For the less advanced countries, with their fearsome problems of runaway population growth and the associated starvation, there can surely be no question of the value of any means of cheapening food, increasing its production, getting rid of waste.

One form of service which a manufacturer can sell to consumers is packaging. This may seem unlikely as one struggles with some of the cleverer modern containers, especially the plastic ones, to get at whatever may be inside, and packaging is apt to arouse the wrath of advanced thinkers as they contemplate the cost it presumably adds to retail prices, the opportunity it provides for meretricious display and misleading advertising, the waste of resources which they consider it entails, and the unmanageable litter it creates. Yet the pack, as William Lever realised over 90 years ago when he started selling Sunlight Soap in wrappers made from specially prepared paper, does offer benefits which are lacking from goods sold loose.

The pack is a guarantee of genuineness; of freshness; of weight (or volume). It checks waste. It saves the shopper's and the shopkeeper's time by getting rid of all the cutting, weighing, wrapping that used to go on. It makes storage much easier and more hygienic. It carries instructions, which some people read. It makes brands much easier to pick off the shelf, which is an advantage to the manufacturer, the retailer and the consumer, becoming ever more

Right: The decoration of ice cream gateaux is brought to a high art—Iglo NV, Netherlands.

Opposite: The Ghana Textile Printing Co.

Pages 70 and 71: Harvesting peas on a large scale for Iglo NV in the Netherlands. Inset: Batchelors in the UK have successfully developed ranges of dried foods to complement their canned food business.

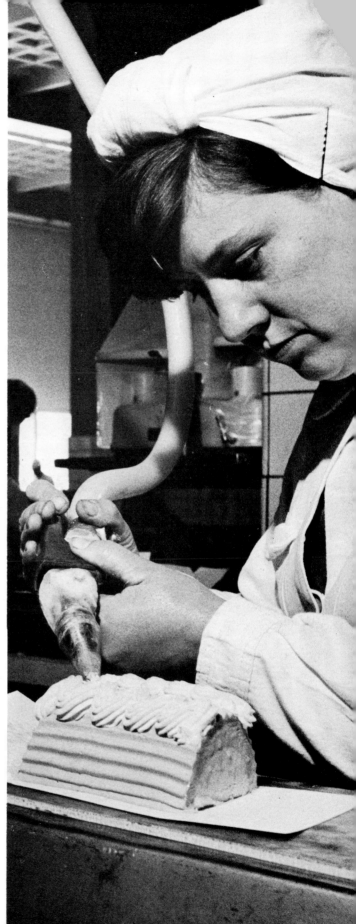

69

Midland Poultry in the UK specialises in the production and processing of chickens and turkeys. The individual, left, tastes as good as he looks.

Below: Their products are sold under the brand name 'Chukie'.

Foot of page: Turkeys being packed at the factory at Craven Arms, Shropshire, UK.

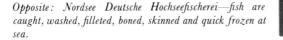

Opposite: *Nordsee Deutsche Hochseefischerei*—fish are caught, washed, filleted, boned, skinned and quick frozen at sea.

important as self-service shopping spreads. The 'retailing revolution' of the last 25–30 years, which has transformed shopping and greatly strengthened the retailers' bargaining power against the manufacturers, would hardly have come about without modern packaging.

Unilever has been in packaging from its earliest days, meaning also printing, since the one goes with the other. Soap and margarine factories in many countries had their printing works, and as well as those there were paper mills in Bavaria, inherited from the Margarine Union, and a large interest in Thames Board Mills, from Lever Brothers. With the rise of modern chemical industry, especially since 1945, the range of packaging materials has widened enormously. Apart from developments in older materials such as glass, metal foil and paper, plastic film of various kinds and rigid plastic containers have come into use, either on

their own or in combination with paper, board, metal and glass. Unilever has taken advantage of this growth and diversity both for the multi-farious needs of its own business and for the opportunities it has offered on the open market. Unilever's packaging interests have grown larger and more widespread, especially in the United Kingdom, where Thames Board Mills, vigorously expanding, were taken over completely in 1964, and in Germany. The formation in 1965 of the '4P' Group—Paper, Packaging, Plastics, Printing—emphasised the importance of these activities in Unilever. Like transport, advertising and market research they have developed from internal services into profit earners on the open market.

Takeover logic in the '60's, fed by optimism, soared far, wide and high, and Unilever responded to the spirit of the times. In packaging it pointed, or seemed to point, towards the

The '4P' companies (Paper, Packaging, Plastics, Printing) in Europe produce a wide range of packaging materials which are sold to many third party customers as well as to Unilever ones.

Opposite: Toilet soap wrappers being printed and (right) aluminium caps being formed.

Below: Margarine packaging has developed to a considerable degree from the wartime pack shown at the back— Netherlands.

Pages 76 and 77: Continuity—No. 5 machine at Thames Board Mills, UK, started production in 1933 and is still going strong. Inset: Nairn Floors, UK. This machine prints floor-covering for seven averaged-sized kitchens every minute.

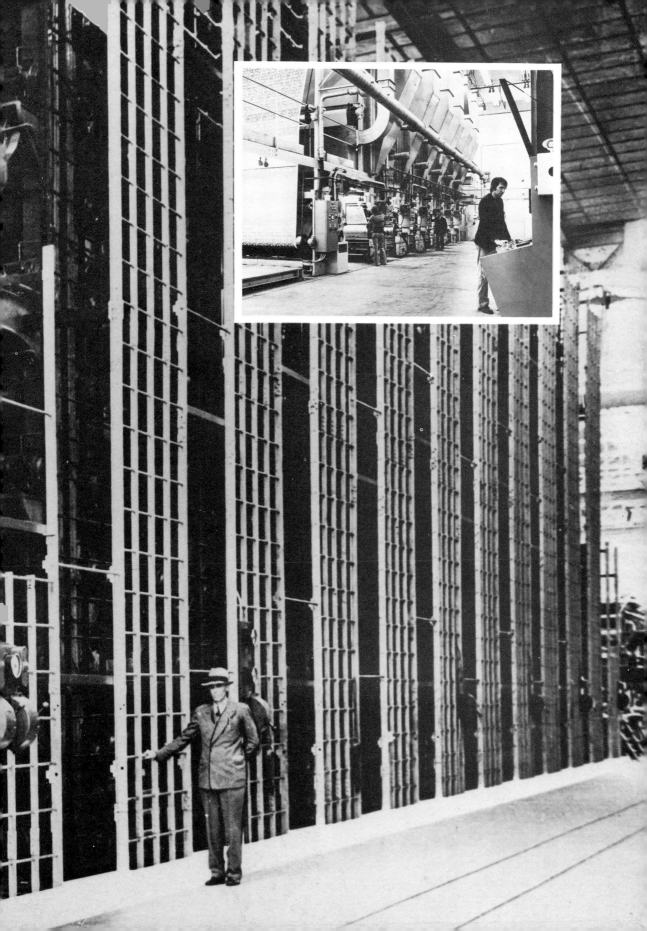

Above: Fine chemicals are produced by Joseph Crosfield and Sons, Warrington, England, for use in many vital industries.

Opposite: Proprietary Perfumes Ltd, England, make perfumes which they sell all over the world. Compounding perfumes demands great skill and knowledge. This picture was taken at Bermondsey before the company moved to Ashford, UK.

fabrication of plastics into flexible packaging: an activity in which Unilever was well established at Forchheim in Germany. In the United Kingdom, Unilever took over E. R. Holloway Limited in 1961, but their business of converting plastics into packaging material and other products is not one in which size necessarily confers an advantage, and in the less hopeful atmosphere of 1974 Holpak Limited, successor to Holloways, was sold to Metal Box.

In 1964 Unilever took a 50 per cent interest in Commercial Plastics, converted three years later into 100 per cent ownership. That represented an even higher flight of corporate imagination, for the business—highly prosperous—relied on forms of plastic sheet which had little or no connection with packaging. One was Fablon, already well established, and the other was a vinyl wall covering called Mayfair. For several years Commercial Plastics' position in Unilever was indeterminate and insecure, but eventually, in August 1975, it was decisively strengthened by the takeover of a complementary business, Nairn Williamson, which had itself been formed by a merger of old-established businesses in floor-coverings and wall-coverings. To the outside eye, it all seems a long way from soap, margarine, convenience foods, and even packaging.

In May 1968, eager for expansion in pharmaceutical products, a field Unilever did not strongly occupy, the Board made a bid worth about £60m for T. J. Smith & Nephew. It was beaten off: an unusual discomfiture for Unilever. Towards the end of 1968, undismayed, the Board advanced on a much bigger objective: Allied Breweries, with over £228m of sales and 22,000 people employed in the United Kingdom alone, as well as large interests on the Continent and elsewhere. The Board of Allied, unlike the Board of Smith & Nephew, were willing and the two companies prepared to merge into a single enterprise which might have been worth some £930m. Before it was actually made, the whole proposal was referred to the Monopolies Commission. That was in January 1969. The Commission raised no obstacles, but by the time they reported, in May, movements in the two companies' share prices had undermined their negotiating position. The project was dropped.

For Unilever the bid for Allied marked the high point of the takeover enthusiasm—or was

it mania?—of the '60's. The argument for it, founded on Unilever's interest in food and, through UAC, in beer and wine, had a certain persuasiveness, but success would have produced a merger of staggering size and complexity. Was it possible to hear, on the fourth floor of Unilever House in May 1969, a faint—*very* faint—but unmistakable sound of blessings being called down upon the unaccustomed head of the Monopolies Commission?

As well as paper, packaging and plastics, Unilever in the '60's and '70's has been cultivating another relatively unfamiliar field: chemicals, meaning chiefly fatty acids, glycerine, vitamins, perfumery and adhesives. Unkind people used to be inclined to say that Unilever wasn't in chemical industry at all, only in cookery, but such truth as there may at one time have been in the gibe has become over recent years progressively less. Technically, Unilever's chemical interests are related to the traditional activities of the business, especially those based on oils and fats, but in marketing they differ widely. Being aimed at industrial customers, they depend not at all on large-scale advertising and associated techniques but very heavily on technical service.

Of all the changes which have come about in Unilever during its 50 years none has been more dramatic than the transformation of its largest subsidiary: the United Africa Company. In 1929, newly formed from the merger of the Niger Company and African & Eastern Trade Corporation, it was largely a merchant company active mainly in Nigeria but also in many other countries in tropical Africa and in the Middle East, most of which seemed to be securely under the rule or protection of one or other of the great imperial powers. Its business consisted chiefly of selling fairly simple European manufactures and in buying produce, so that its profits depended on the terms of trade.

In the years immediately after the war UAC was providing about one-fifth of Unilever's

Opposite: Synthetic adhesives—poly-vinyl-acetate—being made at Silvertown, England.

Right: Giant kettles at Schoonebeek (Netherlands) produce resins for a variety of purposes. The plant is highly automated.

81

turnover and even more—one-third to one-half (together with Plantations Group)—of the profit. Then its traditional business began to come under pressure. Governments in West Africa, still colonial governments, began to set up produce marketing boards which disturbed UAC's buying, and local traders who had formerly acted as produce buyers and as middle men began to set up on their own in the sale of European manufactures. As independence loomed and in more and more colonies became a fact, the pressure hardened. UAC's response, developed from the '50's onward, has been to switch, often with partners outside Unilever, into activities which, with an element of manufacturing or technical service about them, are still beyond local resources but can nevertheless find a market in West African countries, in their export trade or elsewhere.

By 1974 UAC, in partnership with Heineken and Guinness, was in brewing in Ghana, Nigeria, Sierra Leone; in timber, producing sawn timber, blockboard, plywood and other products in Nigeria; in the distribution and servicing of motor vehicles and in similar activities for civil engineering and agricultural machinery, including operations in East Africa;

The transformation of the United Africa Company. Above: Surf boats at Accra, Ghana.

Opposite, top: Tree felling in Ghana for the important timber trade.

Opposite, below: Bottling plant, Nigerian Brewery, at Aba.

in the manufacture and marketing of toilet preparations, proprietary medicines, surgical implements and a range of laboratory equipment developed in Unilever research establishments; in textiles; industrial services; foods; shipping in which Palm Line, wholly owned, was running 12 cargo liners.

From the early '70's, following pressure in some African countries for local participation in foreign enterprises, the share capital of some of UAC's largest subsidiaries has been passing into local ownership. Since the forced sale, at a very low price, of 60 per cent of the equity of its large Nigerian subsidiary, UAC International is no

Above: The United Africa Company diversifies—Kennedys Garden Centre, Swindon, UK.

Opposite, above: Lipton Tea launch in Chile, 1979. Below: The development of packaging. Thames Board Mills products for Unilever and other customers made at Workington, UK.

Above: Lorry assembly, Nigeria.

Opposite: Three generations admire the new technology— Greece.

Pages 86 and 87: The Palm Line plies between West Africa and Europe and here the launch of a new Palm Line vessel is seen by two of her sisters. The Katsina Palm is at anchor, the Kano Palm is being launched and the Enugu Palm is under construction, 1957. Inset: A traditional way of delivery.

longer the majority shareholder of the company but remains associated with the management. Unilever recognises the trend of the times and, provided the price offered for shares is fair and Unilever has some say in how the business is run, these transactions are acceptable. The shareholders change and so do the Boards, but the nature of the business remains much the same. It remains to be seen whether in the long run Unilever will regard a 40 per cent owned company in the same light as one wholly owned.

UAC's traditional spheres of influence have been chiefly in West Africa: also in East Africa, North Africa, and the Middle East. There is no reason why activities of the kind outlined above should not be carried on in Western Europe or elsewhere, and against the background of African politics in the '70's, considerable reason why they should. That is why by 1974 the United Africa Company had become UAC International, the initial letters in the title being

Right: Jam ready for labelling at De Betuwe, Tiel, Netherlands.

non-committal, and why it was engaged, amongst many other things, in the distribution of cars in Yorkshire, in textiles in Hong Kong, and in the wine trade in France. Altogether, in 1974 it was in business in 43 countries, 20 of them not in Africa. UAC International, like the United Africa Company, is still Unilever's largest subsidiary but notice has been given, unobtrusively but firmly, that it is not looking entirely inside Africa for its future prosperity.

When Unilever was formed its business had three main branches: margarine and edible fats, with oil milling closely allied; washing products, mostly soap, also with connections in oil milling; tropical enterprises, chiefly UAC and plantations. These branches are still there, but greatly altered in their nature and diminished in proportion to other activities, especially food. UAC International, it has been shown, is based on a different conception of its purpose in life from that of the United Africa Company. Margarine, once scorned as a poor man's substitute for butter, shows signs of becoming a highly regarded health food for the well-to-do. Washing products, having moved a long way from total dependence on oils and fats as raw materials, are designed more and more for specialised purposes rather than general household tasks. The contributions of the various sides of the business to Unilever's total turnover, distinguishing 'traditional' from 'new' activities, looks something like this:

		Per Cent
Margarine, other fats and oils, dairy produce	26	
Detergents, toilet preparations	19	
UAC International	9	
Animal feeds	6	
Plantations, transport, other interests	6	
Total from 'traditional' activities		66
Food, other than margarine etc	26	
Chemicals, paper, packaging, plastics	8	
Total from 'new' activities		34
Total Unilever turnover, 1977		100

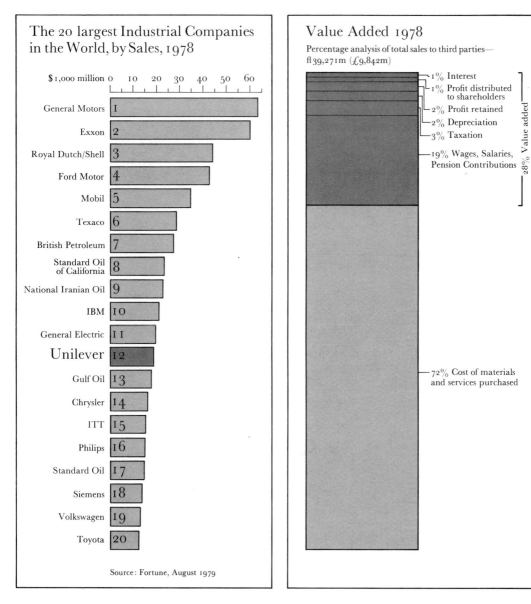

The 20 largest Industrial Companies in the World, by Sales, 1978

$1,000 million 0 10 20 30 40 50 60

General Motors	1
Exxon	2
Royal Dutch/Shell	3
Ford Motor	4
Mobil	5
Texaco	6
British Petroleum	7
Standard Oil of California	8
National Iranian Oil	9
IBM	10
General Electric	11
Unilever	12
Gulf Oil	13
Chrysler	14
ITT	15
Philips	16
Standard Oil	17
Siemens	18
Volkswagen	19
Toyota	20

Source: Fortune, August 1979

Value Added 1978

Percentage analysis of total sales to third parties— fl39,271m (£9,842m)

1% Interest
1% Profit distributed to shareholders
2% Profit retained
2% Depreciation
3% Taxation
19% Wages, Salaries, Pension Contributions

28% Value added

72% Cost of materials and services purchased

About one-third of the turnover comes from activities which, 33 years ago, grouped under 'foods' and 'miscellaneous' (see table on p. 60), provided no more than 12 per cent. If UAC International is transferred from 'traditional' to 'new', as perhaps it should be, the proportion of the turnover derived from activities unknown or negligible in Unilever in its early days rises to 43 per cent. It is a striking shift of emphasis. We must pass to the accompanying changes in the structure and location of one of the world's largest multinational businesses.

Left: The twenty largest industrial companies in the world by sales—1978.

Right: Value added 1978, Percentage analysis of total sales to third parties—fl39,271m (£9,842m).

5.
Multinational Life and Times

Most of the power and wealth in the modern world, and the high standards of living that go with them, are concentrated in a few nations representing a minority of the human race. Elsewhere, vast populations live in poverty, easily excited to envy and suspicion of the rich, under governments increasingly dedicated, it seems, to the destruction of the system which has brought so many of the rich their wealth. The Marxist analysis applied to the economy of early Victorian England can be transferred very persuasively to the international economy of the late 20th century, and Western capitalism finds itself ever more strongly under attack.

Over the last quarter-century the transformation of UAC has reflected the growing power of critics of Western capitalism, and the accompanying change in the geographical distribution of Unilever's activities is a reminder that if a business is to be healthy its requirements are both economic and political. There must be opportunities for growth and a reasonably stable and friendly environment in which growth can take place. The increasing instability and unfriendliness of the African environment, since the end of empires, shows up in the dwindling proportion of Unilever's business which is done in Africa. In the mid-'50's, 25 per cent of Unilever's capital was employed in Africa, 20 per cent of Unilever's sales were made there, and they provided about the same proportion of Unilever's profits. Today all the corresponding figures are between 10 and 15 per cent, roughly speaking.

Europe, by contrast, has been a good home to Unilever since its earliest days, and never more so than in the years of high prosperity which followed the signing of the Treaty of Rome. Between 1958 and 1976 real GNP in the six original member states of the EEC rose by 5 per cent a year: the value of trade between

Opposite: Unilever's interests in West Germany are considerable. They are co-ordinated from this Head Office building in Hamburg.

them, more than three times as fast—by 17 per cent. The EEC is the kind of unobstructed marketing area which the ancestors of Unilever —the Dutch margarine makers and William Lever—no doubt wished for but never really expected to see. In planning production and distribution they always had to take account of tariff barriers, leading them to set up far more factories than were really needed. Within the EEC, production for existing businesses could be concentrated in a smaller number of larger factories: new factories could be sited where they would best serve their expected markets: transport and warehousing could be rationally organised, and it is not accidental that in recent years Unilever's transport interests have been growing. Unilever, a child of Europe, has at last been able to reach out towards its full inheritance.

In this benign atmosphere Unilever's European operations, always large, have grown steadily larger, even though lately the convoluted workings of the Common Agricultural Policy have had unfortunate effects in the meat

A very large amount of money and effort is invested in research. Above: a small 'tea plantation' at Colworth House, Bedfordshire, UK.

Opposite: Hindustan Lever's Research Centre at Andheri, Bombay, India.

trade and have not always been kind to margarine. All aspects of Unilever's business, except those that need the tropics, are represented in Europe and some are exclusively or heavily concentrated there, including animal feeds, chemicals, paper, packaging and transport. Nowhere but in Europe does Unilever go fishing and only there and in one other market— Canada—is it in restaurants. A great deal of Unilever's scientific research is carried on in British and Continental laboratories, employing nearly 1,000 scientists, and in 1977, within the EEC of nine members including Great Britain, Unilever was employing nearly 177,000 people in 200 offices and factories, investing in fixed assets at a rate of £300m a year, spending about £1bn on supplies from farmers and others, paying over £350m in taxation, direct and indirect. In Europe as a whole—EEC and other countries—about 72 per cent of Unilever's capital was employed in 1978 (against 48 per cent in 1955) producing nearly 74 per cent of the sales (59 per cent in 1955) and 68 per cent (62 per cent) of the profits.

Beyond Unilever's securely held European base, one market above all the rest has always seemed supremely desirable: North America. North America has everything: a huge free trade area with excellent communications; advanced technology; ample funds seeking investment; 240 million consumers, most of them affluent and eager for novelty; the most ad-

vanced marketing and advertising facilities in the world to help them in disposing of their affluence. Moreover success in North America confers enormous prestige—and rightly. It is extremely difficult to achieve, especially for foreign firms, not least because of the baffling and excruciatingly slow processes of anti-trust litigation.

Unilever has certainly found North American success elusive, sometimes grasped only to be snatched away, as when a strong position in soap powders was outflanked by Procter & Gamble in the late '40's with the launch of *Tide*. The predecessors of Unilever and Unilever itself have been in the USA and Canada since the 1890's, during the last 35 years or so in a range of activities widening outward from the ancestral business, inherited from Lever, in Lux Flakes, washing powders and toilet soap, especially Lux. Under the impetus of Charles Luckman, President of Lever Brothers Company in

the early post-war years, the United States headquarters moved in the early '50's from Cambridge, Massachusetts, into the Lever building on Park Avenue, New York, a towering success architecturally rather than commercially. Luckman brought Pepsodent into the business and expansion followed, with varying results, into margarine, cosmetics, pet foods, dehydrated soup, ice cream, Lipton's Tea. Not all these ventures were permanent, but Lipton's, run independently from Lever Brothers, became by 1972 the biggest supplier of tea to the retail trade in the United States, and in that year the acquisition of Liptons in the United Kingdom made Unilever's tea business one of the largest of its kind in the world.

Notwithstanding Lipton's success and in spite of more than 80 years' persistence, in 1977 the business in the USA and Canada employed only about 10 per cent of Unilever's capital and produced a rather lower proportion of its sales and profits. These proportions, too, were tending to fall rather than rise, much to the disquiet of the Board. In 1978 came the very ambitious acquisition, for $485m, of National Starch, a business in adhesives, starches and speciality organic chemicals, intended to signal take-off towards a much larger Unilever presence in the American economy. It was followed by the purchase of Lawry's Foods Inc for $66m in July 1979.

Up to now, Unilever's American interests have been valuable less for their size than for the gateway which they open into the most advanced economy on earth, where immense skill and inventiveness are applied in most of Unilever's main fields of activity, especially the whole process of developing and marketing branded consumer goods. Practical experience in America and close acquaintance with American enterprise and ebullience, to say nothing of access to American finance, are likely to remain among the chief contributions made from across the Atlantic to the prosperity of Unilever world-

Left: Lever House, Park Avenue, New York, USA (centre of picture).

Pages 96 and 97: Canada—a 'Fast Food' Drive-in Restaurant, Winnipeg. Inset: Nordzee operate fish shops and restaurants mainly in West Germany and the Netherlands— this new 'Quick' restaurant is at the Lijnbaan, Rotterdam, Netherlands.

95

wide, especially since America is the base for most of Unilever's international competitors.

America has been the birth-place and the test-bed of many of Unilever's major products, from Wall's ice cream in the early 1920's to Birds Eye frozen foods a generation or more later, taking in such things as stripey toothpaste, non-soapy detergents and chicken noodle soup along the way. The costs of product development are immense, and the risks also, for there are many failures, but in a market as large as America they can be widely spread, and the more widely the better, both for the business doing the spreading and for the final consumer, for the spreading of costs lowers the level of prices which the consumer has to pay.

Opposite: Lipton USA have diversified into convenience foods from the original tea business founded by Sir Thomas Lipton. He is seen (inset), beside the grave of the last survivor of the Boston Tea Party.

Right: The recent acquisition of National Starch widens the opportunities for Unilever in the vital North American markets.

The American market is not the end of the matter. For Unilever and its major competitors there is the possibility that a product or a range of products, successful in one part of the world, may be a success also in others, thus spreading costs still further, and indeed if a project is to justify really heavy development expenditure it *must* show promise of wide multinational acceptance. Only large companies, generally speaking, have the resources for development and distribution on this scale, and from the public point of view this is one of the main reasons for justifying the existence of companies as large as Unilever. Without Unilever's resources,

The lively markets in the East provide growing opportunities. Above: The launch of Signal Toothpaste in Malaysia in the early 60's

Left: An advertisement for Blue Band in Indonesia.

Opposite: Clonal oil palm, produced by tissue culture by Unilever Research, to get higher yields of oil. Inset: Research in India—Interior of Research Laboratory.

Opposite page 101: Ice Cream. Its birthplace may be America but it has been brought to a fine art in Europe, as this Sais advertisement in Switzerland shows.

Page 101: Pure vegetable ghee for export from the Netherlands to Arab countries.

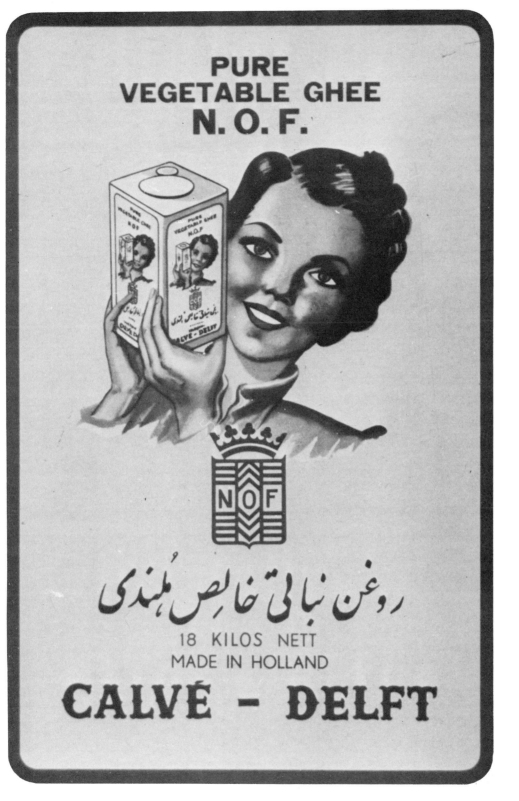

The afternoon concert— and the washing done

With Persil, washing is done almost as soon as breakfast.

You want five minutes to get ready; then Persil takes thirty to make the clothes spotlessly clean. No work, no worry; Persil does it all, and without harm to anything. As soon as the concert starts you can start to listen-in without the faintest feeling of duty neglected, thanks to Persil.

In 3½d and 5½d Packets

Persil is full of oxygen which is set free in the washing. The Persil oxygen eats up the dirt, leaving the clothes clean and unharmed.

Write for free booklet which tells how to use Persil.

...till Uncle dried her eyes on a Persil-washed hankie!

Even you, with all your washing experience, may be mistaken in *thinking* your things are white. See them next to something washed in Persil — the difference will astonish you! Persil's dazzling whiteness makes ordinary washing look positively drab. No wonder; because whereas ordinary washing only gets dirt *off* the fabric, Persil's soap plus oxygen action gets dirt right *out* of the fabric! So, of course, the wash, being perfectly clean, is bound to be extra white. Make *your* next wash a Persil one; you'll never return to ordinary washing!

THE AMAZING OXYGEN WASHER

PER 525

Persil advertising in the UK started before 1930 and has been carefully fostered and developed ever since as the advertisements on the following pages show. Except for a short period in 1969, it has been the market leader in washing powders. (The name Persil is only used by Unilever in the UK and France—elsewhere in Europe it belongs to Henkel.)

Opposite: The 1920's. Above: 1936.

Whose mother hasn't jumped to this year's news about Persil?

ALWAYS tops for whiteness, Persil now has a new quality — a special quality which gives a *radiant, resplendent finish* to white clothes.

Persil perks up tired whites marvellously. It even renews the appearance of those that have become dingy after chancy washings when you couldn't get Persil.

Scientific tests prove that Persil now makes whites up to 7 shades whiter. Persil is best and safest for the whole wash.

PERSIL WASHES 7 shades WHITER

1948.

many of the products discussed in Chapter Four would either not be on the market anywhere or, if anywhere, at luxury prices.

As multinational marketing developed in the rising prosperity of the '50's, after the fragmentation of Unilever during the Second World War, a major problem of organisation began to emerge. Subsidiaries at that time were expected to compete vigorously with each other and 'National Managements' or their equivalent in various countries were encouraged to frame and pursue their own policies, so that a tradition grew up quickly, as traditions have a way of doing, of decentralised control and local initiative, and Unilever companies took pride in it. The importance of the Unilever connexion was played down and often almost forgotten except at the highest levels of company and National Management, and even there it was not always regarded with becoming reverence.

In educating an independent-minded, self-reliant generation of Unilever management the post-war tradition of unemphatic central direction played an important part, though on occasion action could be decisive, as when on a winter day in 1950 Paul Rijkens and Geoffrey Heyworth, described by *Time* magazine as 'two of the world's most potent tycoons', descended on Lever Brothers in the USA and removed the head of the business. For the most part Rijkens and Heyworth as Chairmen, the one of NV, the other of Limited, took the lead in promoting the post-war decentralisation of Unilever. Rijkens retired in 1955, Heyworth in 1960. By that time strains were beginning to show in adapting the established Unilever theory of management to the practice of multinational marketing.

There was in the first place the strain imposed by the pressure of competition, particularly from other great multinational businesses, the most powerful being Procter & Gamble. In these circumstances, internal competition between Unilever companies began to look expensive and pointless. In 1960 the process of rationalisation set on foot in the United Kingdom soap business by Heyworth in the '30's reached its logical conclusion with the concentration of all brands of washing products under the control of a single company: Lever Brothers & Associates. Similar measures were taken in other product fields and in other countries.

Then there was the question how far a National Management might be allowed its own way in the development and marketing of products and ranges of products specifically designed for local needs. Local needs were certainly not to be ignored or wantonly overridden, and there have been major successes such as the development of 'Vanaspati' (vegetable ghee) for the Indian market and the rather similar development in Turkey of edible fats suited to the Turkish market and based on home-grown vegetable oils. But there might easily be waste if Unilever resources were too readily diverted to a multitude of projects of limited application—projects which might well be left to local firms—and there would certainly be waste if resources devoted to major brands were not employed to the full by distributing these brands as widely as possible. Either the negative decision to turn down a local project or the positive decision to introduce an international brand into a national market might require a very nicely judged combination of local consultation with firm central direction and neither decision would be easily reconcilable with the old tradition of local independence. Moreover specialised advice on technology, scientific research, marketing research and marketing technique generally might not be available locally, but it could readily be supplied from Unilever's central services. There is a very thin line indeed between offering advice and giving instructions, and again a degree of firmness might be necessary.

These problems were complex and subtle, requiring for their solution a blend of authority and persuasion, and a marriage between local sensitivity and world-wide advantage which would be very difficult to infuse into the lines and squares of an organisation chart or to express in directives and terms of reference, both of which in any case Unilever generally preferred to leave rather vague. Moreover in any large organisation tension is inherent in the relationship between the centre and the circumference and it is doubtful whether there ever can or ever should be any permanent solution. The balance between the two alters with circumstances and in most large companies with a long history the pendulum swings incessantly, if slowly, between centralisation and devolution.

In a world-wide business such as Unilever runs, there are great economies of scale, redounding to the advantage of the consumer as well as the producer, to be gained from marketing identical brands in all countries. On the other hand it would be unwise to ignore local tastes and prejudices entirely. The balance is difficult to adjust accurately. It may swing towards the brands or towards local interests. In Unilever the post-war system of powerful National Managements loaded the 'local in-

1951.

terest' side very heavily. During the '60's, not without anguish and controversy, a new system of organisation was devised which tilted rather towards universal brands.

The key figure in the new scheme of things, introduced at first tentatively and then with growing assurance, was a personage hitherto unknown in the Unilever hierarchy: the Product Co-ordinator. Each Co-ordinator, as he was appointed—there were three in 1962, six in 1969, ten in 1977—was given general responsibility for the development and welfare of a group of related products. In 1977 the Detergents Co-ordinator, based in London, looked

after 23 companies in 14 countries; the Edible Fats and Dairy Co-ordinator, Rotterdam, 14 in 14; the Frozen Products Co-ordinator, also Rotterdam, 13 in 11, and other Co-ordinators varying numbers of companies in varying numbers of countries. National Managements in Europe grouped under Regional Directors remain. They are responsible for the general Unilever interest and for providing a secure administrative environment within which the companies can get on with their job without distraction. The National Managements particularly look after relations with government and with trade unions, personnel matters, finance and taxation: matters of great and growing importance.

The Product Co-ordinators' strongest influence is within Europe but elsewhere it is strong also, since it makes sound sense, generally speaking, for companies in other markets, mostly smaller, to take advantage of European experience, as Europe often takes advantage of experience in America, and to draw on London or Rotterdam for central services and for mar-

1951–52.

keting and technical support. This is especially true of the detergents business, one-third of which arises 'overseas' (the Unilever word for 'outside Europe') where it has long historical roots, originating from the Lever connection, and where it faces Procter & Gamble's ubiquitous competition which, being centrally co-ordinated, requires a co-ordinated response. Outside Europe, National Managements report as may be appropriate to the Overseas Committee, UAC International or Regional Management North America.

The Product Co-ordinators are members of the Board. From the Board, ultimately, all responsibility and all authority for running Unilever derive their force, however widely they may be decentralised. Legally there are two holding companies, Unilever Limited and Unilever NV, and so there are two Boards, but from the beginning all Directors have belonged

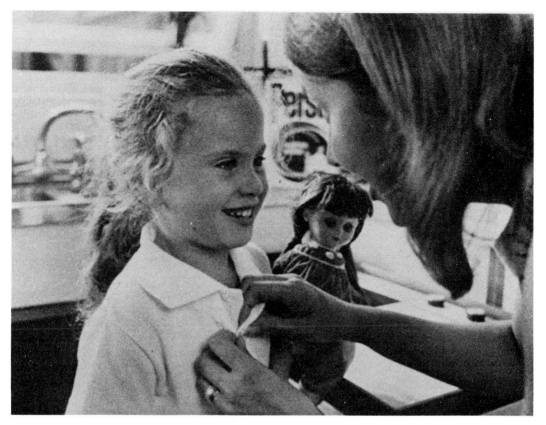

1970's.

to both Boards and the intention has been to run the business as a unity: an intention which as time goes on is increasingly emphasised, to the extent that there is no single head office but two, one in London and one in Rotterdam.

To work effectively, any Board must consist of like-minded individuals who, however much they may disagree on particular issues, can work together in the general interest. Any Board, therefore, and the Board of Unilever is no exception, has something of the nature of a club, in the sense that as a rule new members will only be admitted who are congenial to those already-there. Most large public companies have a number of part-time, non-executive Directors. Unilever, again following a tradition peculiarly its own, has none, the nearest equivalent being the 'advisory directors' who do not share the full powers of the Board.

Of the two dozen or so members of the Board

(23 in 1979) nearly all are primarily departmental managers at a very exalted level, having responsibilities either as Product Co-ordinators or for geographical areas or for specific functions such as finance or personnel management. The only members of the Board who act purely as Directors—that is, giving their undivided attention, without departmental pre-occupations, to the matters of general policy which are the responsibility of the Board as a whole—are those Directors whom their colleagues elect to serve on the Special Committee. It usually consists of the Chairman of Limited, the Chairman of NV and one or two (at present one) other members.

This Committee has at its disposal the entire resources of Unilever, except in so far as its use of them is restricted or directed, and it is increasingly restricted and directed, by various governments. Unilever's resources, it has sometimes been pointed out, are roughly equivalent in money terms to those of a smallish independent state, but the comparison is misleading in all respects except scale because a commercial

Unilever Board SPECIAL COMMITTEE

Functional divisions departments

audit
commercial
corporate development
economics
engineering
financial
information
insurance
legal and secretarial
marketing
market research
organisation
pensions
personnel
research

Product co-ordinations

animal feeds; chemicals; detergents; edible fats and dairy; frozen products; meat products; paper, plastics & packaging; sundry food & drinks; toilet preparations; transport

Regions of operations

Europe

companies in: Austria, Belgium, Denmark, Finland, France, Germany, Greece, Ireland, Italy, Netherlands, Portugal, Spain, Sweden, Switzerland, United Kingdom

Overseas

companies in: Argentina, Australia, Bangladesh, Brazil, Central America, Chile, Colombia, Ghana, India, Indonesia, Japan, Kenya, Malawi, Malaysia, New Zealand, Nigeria, Pakistan, Philippines, Singapore, South Africa, Sri Lanka, Thailand, Trinidad, Tunisia, Turkey, Uganda, Venezuela, Zaire

plantations companies in: Belgium, Cameroon, Ghana, Malaysia Nigeria, Solomon Islands, Zaire

North America

companies in: Canada, USA

Regional managements

Regional managements Europe
National managements

Overseas committee
National managements

Plantations group

Regional management North America

UAC International

operations in:
Arabian Gulf
Australia
Belgium
Benin
Burundi
Cameroon
Canary Islands
Central Afr. Rep.
Chad
Congo
France
Gabon
Germany
Ghana
Hong Kong
Indonesia
Italy
Ivory Coast
Japan
Kenya
Malaysia
Morocco
Netherlands
Niger
Nigeria
Rwanda
Senegal
Sierra Leone
Singapore
Solomon Islands
Tanzania
Togo
Uganda
UK
USA
Zaire
Zambia

enterprise and a state have totally different objectives. A commercial enterprise, for example, does not contemplate making war or re-organising society. It is the duty of the Special Committee to see that the resources of the business, meaning chiefly management and finance, are allocated among the parts of the enterprise so as to achieve the objectives of the whole. In order to do that, it 'sets overall targets, proposes policies and strategies to the Board and monitors progress against the annual and long-term plans'. Its method of working is a ceaseless round of meetings and debate with Directors in charge of Product Groups and regions, with functional Directors, with the Board as a whole, varied for individual members by frequent travelling. The Board as a whole, including the members of the Special Committee, meets once a fortnight, sometimes in London, sometimes in Rotterdam.

The Board arms the Special Committee with formidable powers. It controls the appointment, placing, pay and if necessary dismissal of top managers. It regulates major capital expenditure. To it, for approval, come plans drawn up by management groups. It defines financial and dividend policies. All the Special Committee's powers derive from the Board and to the Board the Special Committee must report, presenting its decisions in the form of recommendations. For practical purposes the Special Committee is the Government of Unilever sustained, like other Governments, by a wide-ranging and powerful bureaucracy.

This majestic administrative engine, with its long history, its traditions, its conventions and —here and there—its mythology, exists to drive profit-earning machinery of which the main moving parts are 500 companies throughout the world carrying, mostly, brand names for their banners. Lux, Omo, Sunlight; Rama, Blue Band, Astra; Langnese, Iglo, Birds Eye; Elida, Gibbs, Denim; these and several hundreds more

Opposite: The 1980 Special Committee of Unilever.

Top: H. F. van den Hoven, Chairman, Unilever NV, (from 1975).

Centre: Sir David Orr, Chairman, Unilever Ltd, (from 1974).

Bottom: K. Durham, Vice-Chairman, Unilever Ltd, (from 1978).

are for most people in most countries the most conspicuous manifestations of Unilever.

The companies are very dear to Unilever's heart, as they should be, considering their central function, but the reverse is not always true when higher authority seems to be obtruding itself undesirably into the conduct of business. Decentralisation is still an article of faith in orthodox Unilever doctrine, but there is a tinge of make-believe about it as there must be if the central authorities are doing their job in directing the parts for the good of the whole. It remains true, nevertheless, that the managers of companies are expected to form their own plans, based on local knowledge, on their own initiative, and then it is for them to convince the central authorities that what they want to do is worth doing, rather than for the central authorities to lay down, except in broad terms, what the companies must do.

Unilever's power over many of its companies is qualified more or less severely by the presence of partners holding a greater or lesser share of the capital: a development which has gathered pace during the past 30 years or so and was certainly not foreseen in anything like its modern strength by the founders of the business. Some partners have been sought for and willingly admitted to the running of joint enterprises such as the chemical business Unilever-Emery of Gouda or the projects undertaken with Heineken and Guinness. Other partners have been accepted with greater or lesser reluctance because governments, chiefly in ex-colonial territories, have insisted. Since what will be, will be, Unilever today is not disposed to quarrel, provided that a fair price is offered and that arrangements for management remain satisfactory to Unilever.

When Unilever was founded, 50 years ago,

Left: Unilever-Emery, Netherlands, water purification.

Above: Training is vital and wide-spread. At a recent Margarine Course in the Netherlands, managers from over 20 different countries attended.

key positions in Europe and elsewhere were usually held by Dutchmen or Englishmen, but in the mid-'30's the process known in Unilever as 'isation'—Indianisation, Africanisation and so on—began. Positions of authority were progressively transferred to locally born managers, leaving to expatriates only positions requiring special knowledge or training not at the time locally available. In developing countries, as early as 1966, some 92 per cent of the managers were home grown, and Dutch accountants and English marketing men, at one time widespread in European countries other than their own, passed gradually from the scene. Nowadays, on the principle that a judicious mixture of nationalities adds sparkle, there is a conscious policy of appointing some proportion of managers—at present about 7 per cent of the

total—to jobs outside their own countries, provided other countries will receive them. Most of these expatriate managers have so far been European, but there is a rising proportion of Asians, Africans and Latin Americans among them. On the Board five nationalities are represented, and the arrival there in 1979 of an Indian, Mr T. Thomas, may perhaps be seen as crowning 'isation' with an appointment from the country where it all began, over 40 years ago.

Of the 318,000 people employed by Unilever about 20,000 are managers, spread over 75 countries. For many of them Unilever is their world, in which they spend all or the greater part of their careers, referring to the rest of the universe as 'outside'. In a moderately successful working life a manager will move from job to job in his own country or perhaps in others, meeting and mixing with managers from other parts of the business and from other countries at conferences, on visits and on training courses.

Unilever spends a great deal of money—about £100m a year—on training, and of that sum about one-third is spent on the managers. About one manager in five gets some kind of formal training every year, not necessarily confined to the junior levels of the business or to the earliest phases of his career.

Management selection, in Unilever, places emphasis on good rather than superlative intelligence and on ability to co-operate. The eccentric or the awkward customer, however brilliant, even if selected, has no very high survival rate within the business. As is probably inevitable, even desirable, in a long-established, very large enterprise, the successful Unilever manager needs the skill of the professional administrator as well as the outlook of the business man.

Similarity of selection and experience sets up a process of indoctrination, not entirely deliberate, through which a Unilever manager, if his career is going well, finds himself after some years a member of an unacknowledged club for many nationalities and both sexes in which the sense of identity and the force of unspoken tradition, as in most good clubs, is strong. It gives Unilever management throughout the world a character and a style which is very marked, though not easy to describe. Thoroughness and professional competence, rather than entrepreneurial brilliance, seem to be its leading characteristics, joined to an outlook generally liberal and humane, often self-questioning, and an awareness, not to say uneasiness, about the social responsibilities of multinational business. 'We are in business for a long time' one highly-placed Unilever manager used to say, and that perhaps sums up the aims and nature of Unilever managers as well as any eight words could do.

In training managers Unilever, like other well-conducted multinationals, does a service to the economy of any country where its companies are in business. In Europe immediately after the Second World War Unilever played a part in bringing in American management methods greatly to European advantage, and since then there has been a wider dissemination of 'best practice', valuable especially in developing countries. Each year over 300 overseas managers come to Europe on training courses, training goes on overseas, and by 1979 men from 24 countries had been sent to USA on six-month marketing attachments. 100 senior managers of many nationalities have attended the Harvard Advanced Management Programme at Unilever's expense. Managers trained by Unilever do not all stay with

'Four Acres', Kingston-upon-Thames, UK, allows training to take place in pleasant relaxed surroundings throughout the year.

Unilever, for the training which they have had is exceedingly marketable, and they can easily find employers anxious for them to practice what has been preached. That is sad—and expensive—for Unilever, but it is a bonus for the economy.

Unilever touches the community at so many points—as employer, as buyer, as seller, as advertiser, as borrower of funds, as consumer of resources, as taxpayer, as polluter—some say—of the environment—and its power is appar-

ently so great that it attracts attention, wherever it goes, not only from Governments but from political parties, churches, trade unions, pressure groups of many kinds seeking to influence opinion. Power not only attracts attention. It generates fear. 'There is the fear', said Sir Ernest Woodroofe in 1973, 'that the national Government will be impotent against this power. All our experience testifies to the reality of these fears. Equally, it testifies to the lack of justification for them.'

Does it? A great many people, not all of them ill-informed or politically biased, would disagree. Nor is suspicion of multinationals peculiar to countries where they are foreigners. It is prevalent also in Unilever's home countries.

What then is Unilever? Is it a beneficent provider of essentials for the multitude, or a sinister tool of international capitalism, wringing exorbitant profits from the poor for the benefit of the wealthy?

After this survey of 50 years' development, it may be well to stand back and try to take a balanced view.

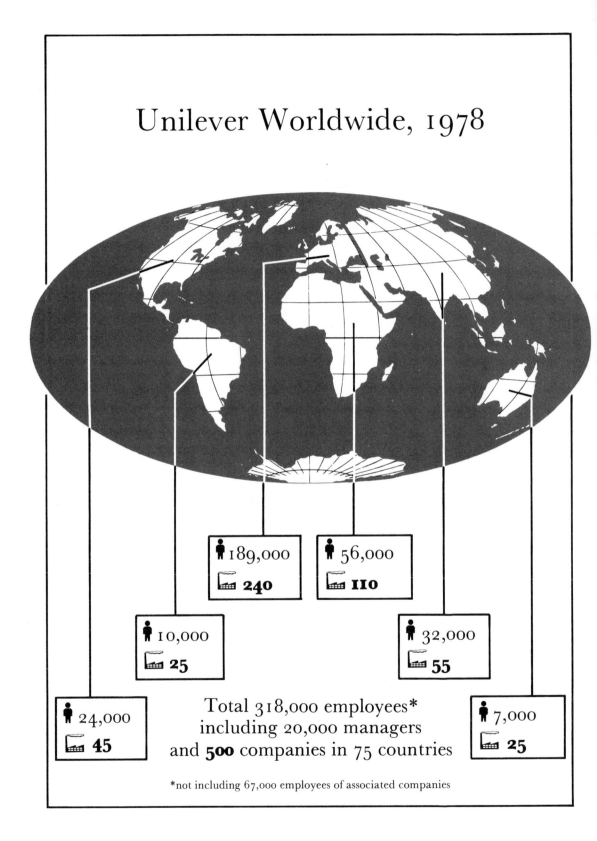

Unilever Worldwide, 1978

189,000
240

56,000
110

10,000
25

32,000
55

24,000
45

Total 318,000 employees*
including 20,000 managers
and **500** companies in 75 countries

7,000
25

*not including 67,000 employees of associated companies

6.
Unilever at Fifty

O ne thing is certain. Unilever is a wealth machine. Wealth goes in at one end and greater wealth comes out at the other. The wealth that goes in is in the form of materials and services: the wealth that comes out is in the form of marketable products, and it is generated by the work done in Unilever companies and departments throughout the world: work in research, development, distribution, marketing, accountancy and general management as well as in manufacturing. The value of this work in 1978 amounted to rather more than a quarter of the total value of Unilever's sales, as shown in the table on the following page. This sum of £2,738m may fairly be regarded as the measure of wealth created by Unilever in that year.

The wealth created by Unilever does not remain stagnant, nor does it flow to a narrow circle of wealthy capitalists: indeed quite the contrary. In 1978 £1,839m— 67 per cent of the total value added—was paid in wages, salaries and pension contributions to 318,000 people who were working for Unilever and its subsidiaries during the year, giving an average of £5,783 each. The element of profit in the value added is quite small—£609m in 1978—and of that, by the time Governments throughout the world had taken what they considered to be their share, £294m was left for Preference and Ordinary shareholders—the capitalists* —but of that they only received £127m in cash because the Board decided to hold back £167m to finance the development of the business.

The shareholders are not a small group. In NV it is impossible to say how many there are because their names are not registered, but in Limited there are nearly 79,000 of them, as the first table overleaf shows. The largest shareholder, the

---

* Holders of loan stock and other lenders are also capitalists. They received £116m interest before profits were calculated.

UNILEVER LIMITED—OWNERSHIP OF ORDINARY CAPITAL 1978

Shareholders		% of total		Nominal Value £m
Leverhulme Trust	1		18	8.4
Insurance companies	870	16		
Pension funds	257	5		
Other financial institutions	4,759	5		
			26	12.0
Nominee companies	3,813	27		
Other companies	1,225	5		
			32	14.5
Individuals	67,870		24	10.9
Total Holders	78,795		100	45.8

VALUE ADDED TABLE

	£ m	%
Unilever sales to third parties, including associated companies	9,958*	100
Cost of materials and services purchased	7,220	
Value added by work done in Unilever	2,738	27·5

* Sales—£9,842m: 'other income' £116m.

Leverhulme Trust, is bound by the terms of the first Lord Leverhulme's will, a complex document.

About 25 per cent of the Trust's income is distributed in support of some 500 projects of scholarly research. Of the beneficial owners of the nominee companies, holding an average of £3,221 (nominal) each, it is obviously impossible to say anything. About half the Ordinary capital is in the hands of individuals and financial institutions. Individual holdings are nearly all small—85 per cent £250 nominal or below—but that says nothing about the wealth of individual holders because many of these small holdings may be part of larger portfolios. At the other end of the scale, in 1978 two individuals held, between them, £233,108 nominal.

The financial institutions, especially the insurance companies and pension funds who hold over 20 per cent of the total, represent the interests of a great many people, certainly running into millions, of whom the majority are unlikely to think of themselves as 'capitalists' although their welfare in old age is heavily dependent on the continued success of capitalism.

The wealth created by Unilever is distributed widely through the world, roughly according to the general pattern of Unilever's structure and activities. Thus the two holding companies are British and Dutch and it appears that most of their shareholders are British and Dutch also, for in 1978 the holders of over 99 per cent of Limited's Ordinary shares had addresses in the United Kingdom and 55 per cent of NV's final dividend was paid in the Netherlands. If, as the last figure suggests, something like 45 per cent of NV's capital is held away from the Netherlands, that is no doubt partly the result of the strenuous efforts which have been made for some years to widen the geographical spread of investment in Unilever. It is impossible to say with any accuracy where the foreign-owned shares are held because 21 per cent of the final dividend was paid in Switzerland, which might mean anything, but the other countries where some portion of the NV dividend was paid were:

Germany	7 per cent
United Kingdom	4
United States	4
France	4
Belgium	3
Other countries	2

Outside shareholders in subsidiaries and associated companies, who are now very numerous, are scattered world-wide, especially in Africa and Asia. Thus 20 per cent of the Unilever com-

Opposite: South African adaptation of a US toothpaste advertising campaign.

"If my dream guy doesn't notice me in this fabulous hairstyle, I'll be sure he's blind."

"Gee, you look gone in that hairstyle, Lindiwe. Now I think you should put your money where your mouth is."

"Here, try Close-up. It's a red toothpaste because it contains mouthwash for your breath."

"Your dream guy is bound to notice you Lindi because Close-up will give you fresh, fresh breath and pure white teeth."

Lindi's costly plaits gave her a film star look, but it's Close-up that brought her dream guy closer.

"Hmm...Close-up I love you."

Put your money where your mouth is. Buy Close-up.

Now with FLUORIDE

LINTAS CB/19161/FPFC

EMPLOYEES OF UNILEVER AND SUBSIDIARIES* 1978

	Number of Employees '000		Proportion of total %
Europe	189		
USA and Canada	24		
	——	213	67
Africa	56		
Asia, Australia, New Zealand	39		
Central and South America	10		
	——	105	33
Total		318	100

* The number employed by associated companies is 67,000, of whom 53,000 are employed in Africa.

pany in Turkey is owned there; 21 per cent of Nippon Lever Industries is owned in Japan; 35 per cent of Hindustan Lever, in India; 40 per cent of Plantations Lever au Zaïre, in Zaïre; 55 per cent of Lever Brothers Ghana Limited, in Ghana; and 60 per cent of UAC of Nigeria, in Nigeria.

About 60 per cent of the people who work for Unilever and its subsidiaries are in Europe, reflecting the volume of business done there, and another 7 per cent are in North America. What proportion of the total wage bill is paid in these areas is not revealed in the published figures, but it must have a considerable influence on the high average figure of wages paid. Outside Europe and North America, Unilever employed 56,000 people in Africa—18 per cent of the total —in 1978, and associated companies, almost as many again (53,000); 39,000 were employed in Asia and Australasia, and 10,000 in Central and South America—see table above.

If most of the wealth created by Unilever flows, as wages and salaries, towards those who work in the business, and relatively little, as dividends, towards those who own the capital, what can we say of other benefits of ownership? Ownership and the wealth and power alleged to go with it lie after all very close to the heart of capitalist free enterprise, the system which brought Unilever into being.

Let us dispose, first of all, of the idea of growing rich through owning Unilever shares. It is

Opposite, above: Unilever Export launches Rexona in Freetown, West Africa. Below: Atkinsons perfumes have long been established in Italy.

possible, of course, to make short-term gains by well-timed speculation, which is undoubtedly what some stockholders hope to do and a few succeed in doing, but the possibility of loss is at least equally great. Leaving speculators out of account, what, in general terms, may the long-term investor in Unilever stock expect to gain?

'Our long-term aim', said the Chairman of NV in January 1979, 'is to continue to grow in real terms at roughly the same rate as in the past.' That rate had averaged 4–5 per cent a year, giving 50 per cent in ten years. He added that he hoped 'to achieve a return on capital employed which would enable us to finance our growth and the inflation from our cash flow'. A business which grows by 50 per cent in real terms in ten years, finances growth largely from its own self-generated wealth, and still pays dividends can hardly be said to be stagnating.

Another Director, on the same occasion, indicated slower growth in Europe in the future, perhaps 2–3 per cent on average, and faster growth 'overseas': that is, chiefly in developing countries—and, of course, the rainbow's end would continue to be chased in the United States. He hoped to see improved products— 'new soft and health margarines' in Europe, for example—but he did not expect to develop radically different ones. 'Apart from the United Africa Group', he said, 'we are still predominantly a detergents business overseas,' and in Unilever's traditional activities he thought there would be considerable scope for extension as purchasing power rose. 'In total', he said, 'the picture of Unilever strategy . . . is . . . character-

THE NEW YORK

CORNERSTONE OF A

STOCK EXCHANGE

PEOPLES CAPITALISM

ised by stability, by continued growth with the total economy and by a conservative financial policy.'

In short, what the Ordinary shareholder in Unilever may expect, provided he does not need to sell at a bad moment, is a reasonably safe home for his money, spread all over the world and buttressed by a great variety of products, domestic and industrial, all of which are unlikely to go into decline at the same moment. If there are failures, as from time to time there are bound to be, the resources of Unilever are large enough to absorb them. When there is success it will be reflected in the growth rate. Nothing can be guaranteed, but if the corporate plan succeeds, both the income from a shareholding and its capital value will keep ahead of

inflation, increasing not merely in money value but in real terms. The investor in Unilever is unlikely to experience the splendours of capitalism, but he may hope to escape its worst miseries also.

The ownership of capital and the exercise of power, 100 years ago, were closely linked, and linked they still may be in companies up to a certain size, not necessarily small, but in companies as large as Unilever they have long moved far apart, simply because the likelihood of one owner or a small group controlling more than a very tiny fraction of the capital (the Leverhulme Trust is a freak) is remote. If nevertheless the business ran so deeply into trouble as to rouse strong feelings, the shareholders would have means of making their sentiments known,

Opposite: Unilever shares are introduced on the New York Stock Exchange.

Below: Cornetto has been one of Europe's success stories—this Italian advertisement shows it.

Pages 120 and 121: Lever Bros, Thailand—a salesman serves his customers by boat. Inset: HB Ice Cream, one of Unilever's Irish subsidiaries, manufactures ice cream and acts as distributor for Birds Eye products. Here representatives of HB present two Thai elephants—appropriately named 'Coffee' and 'Walnut'—to the Zoological Gardens, Dublin.

though they would find it difficult to force an unwilling Board to take account of them or to change the composition of the Board. Like the power of voters in a democracy, the power of shareholders in Unilever is collective, not individual, but that is not to say it does not exist. Apart from formal protest, if the shareholder no longer has confidence in the company it is in his power to sell out, and no Board likes to see too much selling of that sort.

Ownership, in businesses as large as Unilever, has lost most of its traditional attributes. Is it realistic, then, to apply the term 'ownership' at all? Can any group of people, any institutions, be said to 'own Unilever' in any but the formal legal sense? And when this 'ownership', such as it is, is distributed so widely among the

Cornetto Algida
cuore di panna

Algida, voglia di gelato

ALGIDA

public of so many different countries, is it reasonable to go on referring to Unilever as *private* enterprise, except to distinguish it from enterprises that belong to the State? And 'belonging to the State', it may be thought, is not at all the same as being owned by the public.

Unilever, as a multinational corporation, is answerable to public authorities not in one country only but in every country where it operates. Governments everywhere are taking more and more power to regulate business activities 'in the public interest'. This power manifests itself in the control of prices, of profits, of foreign exchange, of imports and exports; in the protection of employment, in wage bargaining, in relations with trade unions. It is applied in the interest, real or supposed, of the consumer and with gleeful censoriousness to advertising. It guides businesses to regions where they would not otherwise establish themselves and sometimes away from regions where they would. It forces the disclosure of information once, no doubt mistakenly, considered private. It is brought to define and forbid pollution and to take care of what is grandly and unspecifically termed 'the environment'.

Some intervention is no doubt beneficial, seeking to bring average practice up to the level of the best. Unilever and other large companies have anticipated a good deal of it, especially in advertising, accounting and the disclosure of information, and perhaps most of all in employment policies, especially pension schemes, which have usually been ahead of their time. Companies like Unilever are certainly no less anxious than governments to make sure—in their own interest—that no harm comes to consumers

from their products. It does sometimes seem, though, that governments are more anxious to prevent companies doing what they should not than to encourage them to get on with what they should. As the Chairmen of Limited and NV observed of anti-pollution measures in 1973, 'There is a limit to what a company can afford.'

If Unilever has public responsibilities on the scale that governments seem to assume, has it also corresponding public power? The assumption seems to be that it has, and that it can hardly be trusted to use it aright, otherwise such elaborate regulation would hardly be necessary.

Anxiety probably hangs thickest over the company's power to employ—and disemploy: power which it must exercise if it is to dispose its resources efficiently. This is bad enough if a company is an employer only in one country, but with a multinational like Unilever there is always the uneasy knowledge that operations may be closed down in one country and opened, or enlarged, in another. Nor can Unilever deny that such things do happen, though the Board may go to great lengths to neutralise their effects on the employees concerned, as when the manufacture of jam for Germany was transferred to the Netherlands, but the people who used to make the jam in Germany were provided with

Opposite: Starting from the days of Lord Leverhulme, plantations have been developed in West Africa and the Far East—this is the Calabar Oil Palm Estate, Nigeria.

Below: A wide range of meat products from Germany.

work on frozen food in the same factory. Such arrangements, however, are not always possible, and the process may be harsh. 'The restructuring of the meat businesses in the Netherlands', says the 1978 Report and Accounts, 'made good progress. Savings resulting from the reorganisation reduced losses.' This rather colourless piece of official prose conceals several years of effort on the part of management and unions alike to make 1,800 jobs disappear as painlessly as possible but not all the effort in the world could entirely anaesthetise such surgery.

Measures like the Protection of Employment Act in the United Kingdom and even stricter

measures elsewhere may make dismissal difficult. Large redundancy payments may soften the blow for those who are dismissed. Early retirement may sometimes be welcome. There is more to a job than livelihood, however, for self-respect and a sense of identity go with it. It is probably fear of the power of dismissal, more than anything else, which gives force to the demand for those who work in a business to have some say in the way it is run.

The demand is not unreasonable. In Germany it appears to have been very successfully met. It has not been so successfully met in the legislation of other countries and for Unilever,

active so widely, it is a demand that is very difficult to meet with that degree of success everywhere. Companies in different countries deal with the matter in different ways as law and custom require, but what may seem desirable to employees in one country may seem totally undesirable to employees elsewhere, and with good reason. Moreover although the safeguarding of employment may loom large in the minds of those employed, there are many other considerations which the Board must take account of in planning the welfare of Unilever as a whole, and on that, in the end, all employment within Unilever depends.

In 1973 the Department of Economic and Social Affairs of the United Nations Secretariat prepared a report to assist the Group of Eminent Persons who were then enquiring into the activities of multinationals. 'The Report', said a Unilever commentary on it, 'is permeated by the suggestion that the multinational is a threat to national sovereignty.' The suggestion is no doubt made most strongly in countries recently under foreign rule, but in one form or

All these Vim packs are produced in the Netherlands, mainly for export. Great care is taken to devise packs exactly suited to each different market.

Lipton's Cup-A-Soup, an overnight success when introduced in the USA.

another it is universal. Just after the British General Election of 1979, a left-wing MP said that multinationals 'literally controlled the economy'. He is not the only one who thinks like that: nor are all who agree with him on this point on his side in politics.

Multinationals are suspect in their home countries. Why invest capital abroad? Why not use it to provide employment here? Exporting goods is held to be virtuous: exporting capital is sinister. The pull of the world's economic development, however, has long been in the direc-tion of local production and away from export trade, and resistance to the tendency would be impossible.

The decision whether or not to put up plant in another country, in response to this tendency, is one of the most serious decisions any Board ever has to face. A decision against amounts to leaving a market open for others to develop. A decision to go ahead means tying up capital, probably for good, in an alien territory. Once a company is established in any country, owning property, plant, vehicles and all the para-phernalia of an active business, it is a prisoner there. A prisoner, no doubt, in easy, even enviable, circumstances so long as things go

Above: Swiss products.

Pages 128 and 129: TMS Birgitta, one of the ships of the modern German shipping operation, 'Elbe' Transport-Union. Inset: Norfolk Line operates roll-on, roll-off ships across the North Sea.

well, but if things go ill very much the reverse, for there is no way of getting capital out again except by selling the assets, and in anything like a forced sale, including expropriation on dictated terms, they are unlikely to realise anything like their true value.

It is this consideration chiefly which makes nonsense of the notion that a company investing overseas is likely to spawn an overmighty subject able to set a host government at defiance. Those who run a company, in dealing with a government—any government, including the one at home—have power mainly in a negative sense: they can refuse to invest. Even that power is at its strongest before the initial investment

NORFOLK FERRY SERVICE

NORFOLK LIJN   NORFOLK LIJN   NORFOLK LIJN

DUKE OF HOLLAND

has been made. After that, a management dis-
satisfied with conditions in any market can refuse to add to its investment there, but to any
management with an eye to growth that is likely
to be a most unwelcome decision, and it may in
itself lead to trouble both with organised labour
and with the government.

The balance of power in a sovereign state is
loaded heavily, as it should be, in favour of the
Government and against any private corporation. The Government decides whether to admit
foreign investment at all, and on what terms,
and G. D. A. Klijnstra, when Chairman of Unilever NV, told the Eminent Persons: 'It is nonsense to claim that we . . . would consider
starting up against the wishes of the local
Government or without fitting our plan into the
country's industrialisation plans.' The Government imposes taxation, both personal and corporate, and it is often arranged—as, for instance,
in the United States, the citadel of free enterprise—to discriminate against foreign investors.
Governments fix the regulations under which
expatriate managers may work, and Unilever
has often found permits very tightly controlled.
A multinational's subsidiary may be permitted
to make profits, but it by no means follows
either that dividends may be freely declared—
their amount is limited in Central America and
the countries of the Andean Pact, to say nothing
of the United Kingdom until recently. Nor does
it follow that, having been paid, they will be
allowed to leave the country. The Government
of Ghana has habitually interfered with the
remittance of profits, though making sure that
dividends due to itself are paid promptly. If a
company seeks to be paid for services rendered,
fees may be refused or limited, as from time to
time they have been in certain countries.

Licences for expansion may be withheld;
production may be limited by quota; prices
may be held down to a level which drives a
company into losses. The anti-trust laws of the
United States set a formidable obstacle course
in the path of companies trying to expand by
takeover. A foreign company may be compelled
to accept local participation on very poor terms:
the price set some years ago for a large holding
in a major African subsidiary represented a
price: earnings ratio of less than two. Finally, a
government may take over the subsidiary of a
foreign corporation entirely, and the terms will
depend on the government's goodwill or lack of
it. Unilever companies have been nationalised
in 17 countries on terms varying from full compensation, as in Iraq, to none at all. In some
cases, compensation has been promised but not
yet paid.

In this unequal situation politics are full of
peril. A working relationship with politicians
and officials must be built up, but from a mere
instinct for self-preservation, if from no higher
motive, any management with international
responsibilities is likely to insist that subsidiaries abroad behave as good, even extra-
good, citizens of the countries where they are in
business. Such exceptions as there may have
been to this rule have not been in Unilever.
Unilever managers are encouraged to con-

*Various activities in support of Rama Margarine. Right:
South Africa. Far right: Japan. Below: Germany.*

Just one bite and you'll find that new Rama has even more of that natural fresh taste than ever before. And it's so good for you, too, because it's made of only the purest vegetable oils and contains vitamins A and D. So lay it on thick.

Just one bite and you know you're right!

New Rama.
Even more of that natural fresh taste.

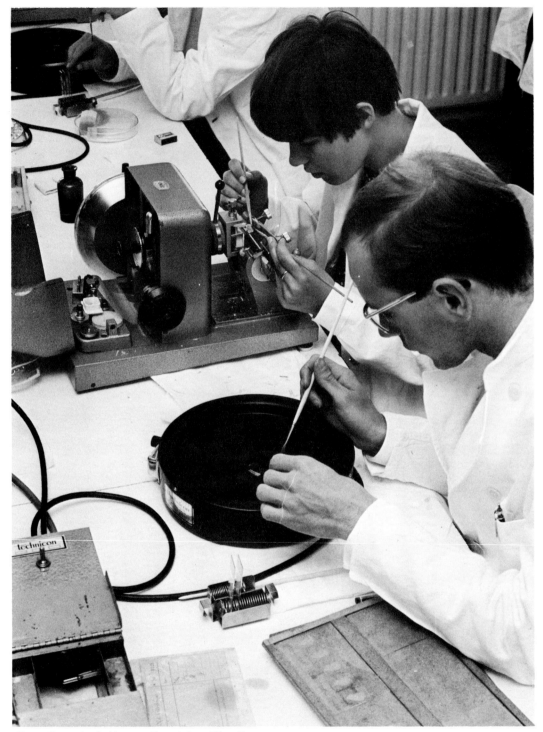

Above: Research—looking at oils and fats, Vlaardingen, Netherlands.

Opposite: Unilever Computer Systems.

Above: Calvé—quality control of cocktail nuts.

Opposite: A traditional kitchen set off by cushioned vinyl from Nairn Floors. Here, the Jedburgh pattern from the 4-metre range.

Maturing cheeses before processing and packing, Baasrode, Belgium, 1962.

Ready for a promotion of Milkana Cheese in Italy, early 1960's.

tribute to the public life of the countries where they work, perhaps by serving on committees of the local Federation of Industries, or of a professional association, or on the Court of a university or business school.

Unilever and other multinationals have not arisen from any kind of conspiracy to wield political power or revive dead empires. Nor have they been thrust upon unwilling societies by the sinister but irresistible force of capitalism. They have arisen because a great many people in all parts of the world, rightly or wrongly, for good reason or bad, want the material equipment of a rich industrial society, all the way from synthetic detergents and fish fingers to sophisticated electronic gadgetry. And they—or their Governments—want as many of these things as possible to be made in their own countries, not brought in from abroad.

Goods are not imported but capital, technology and managerial skill are. All, in time, become part of the economic and social structure of the receiving community, as does the business itself. Nominal ownership of capital may remain, at least in part, in foreign hands but we have seen the limitations on powers of ownership and a going concern is not a piece of movable property which can somehow be spirited away to suit the foreigners' conveni-ence. It remains to distribute wealth widely among the community and to generate employment and secondary business activity, particularly among suppliers and customers, all round it. The running of the business passes steadily into local hands, and managers trained to international standards pass through into other employment. A Chairman of the Indian State Trading Corporation, a Chairman of Hindustan Steel and a chief consultant to the Indian Planning Commission have all come from a Unilever background.

There is no ground for assuming that multinational corporations, whether they invest in the advanced countries of Europe and North America or in the countries of the Third World, are invariably seeking in some way to 'exploit' the 'host nations'. That could not possibly be in their interest, which lies in a healthy economy supporting a rising standard of living, and that is especially true of Unilever. What Unilever seeks is a reasonable return, over a long period of time, on a sound and growing investment.

This is strictly a capitalist outlook. It assumes a market economy in which demand is allowed reasonably free play and those who supply the demand are entitled to take their reward by way of a fair profit. On the wisdom of the demand it makes no judgment, but there is an underlying assumption that even if ordinary people may not know what is good for them, they have a better right to try to find out, at their own risk and expense, than anyone else has to tell them.

In the heyday of American world supremacy after the Second World War, and in the early self-confident period of the EEC, the capitalist outlook was far more widely accepted than in the gloom of the middle and late '70's. Growth is faltering and the linked, intractable problems of over-population and poverty lend weight and passion to the advocacy of Marxist alternatives. In particular it is suggested that multinational corporations pursue the wrong aims in the wrong way. They export, it is said, high technology requiring elaborate capital equipment, whereas what is required is simple technology using abundant labour: a charge to which Klijnstra replied that 'an experienced international company would not be that foolish' and by pointing out that Unilever in India deliberately chose technology requiring 48 man hours to produce a ton of soap, whilst in New Zealand 9 man hours were sufficient.

Multinationals, their critics say, produce for a well-to-do minority rather than meeting the urgent needs of the majority who are in misery. They perpetuate a system which, to quote one American radical, 'concentrates control and power in a few metropolitan centres, leaving the rest of the world as a vast hinterland with a stunted capacity to plan for its future and to fulfil its hopes. It thus maintains and intensifies the system of dependency and misery that now characterises our world economy and accounts for so much of its difficulties and injustices.'

Whether those who run multinational businesses, faced everywhere with irresistible concentrations of power in government hands, would agree with this analysis of the situation is doubtful. They might be more disposed to think Professor C. H. Wilson right in his opinion that 'in these days what the large business possesses is not power but only the appearance of power'. Moreover, while agreeing that a market economy is inclined to overvalue trivia, they might ask whether any system that does not depend on the market has yet done better in supplying necessities. For a century or more private capitalism, working nationally and internationally, has not only produced wealth on an unprecedented scale but has distributed it ever

SPD warehouse full of Unilever products at Chullora, Australia.

137

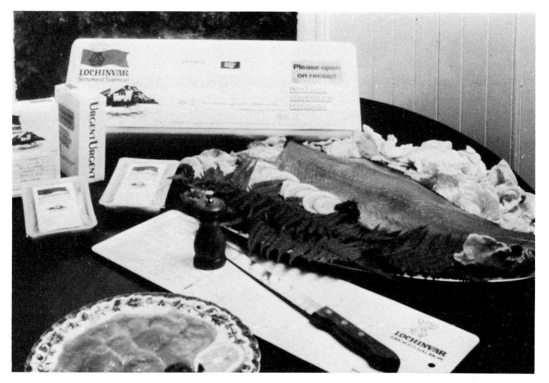

Opposite: Smoking fish, Germany.

Above: Marine Harvest Ltd is a leader in the development of farming of salmon and salmon trout in Scottish lochs. The picture is of Lochinvar smoked salmon and mail order products.

more widely, both geographically and socially. It has not abolished poverty but it has raised a great many people out of it.

In the centre of this process—raising the standard of living—for the last 50 years has been Unilever. Among the large businesses of the world (it ranks in total assets employed 26th: in sales 12th), Unilever is unique. There are oil companies, there are car companies, there are chemical companies, there are food, detergent, toilet-preparations companies, but there is only one Unilever: only one group of companies which makes more margarine than anyone else in the world; sells frozen foods, soup, tea, meat, washing powder, plastic packaging: runs tropical plantations and a shipping line; once tried to break into the market for copying machines (Unilever is always optimistic); is hopefully developing a business in distributing hanging garments; carpets floors and covers walls . . .

and does all these things and many, many more with a bland confidence that they are all the most natural things in the world for it to do, although at the beginning of 1979 a Director did go so far as to say 'we consider Unilever sufficiently diverse in its product coverage.' He then added: 'On the other hand, we do not think that we are too diversified.' Not too little, not too much, but just right.

Perhaps nobody but the English and the Dutch, those two most matter-of-fact of nations, could have issued such a challenge to all the laws of probability and commercial logic as Unilever. The challenge having been issued and maintained for 50 years, however, why should it not indefinitely continue? Unilever is multinational not only in its operations but in ownership and management also, so that wherever Unilever companies are established they are bedded firmly into the economy and society. Rather the same may be said of Unilever's products: articles of daily use and minor luxuries, part of the pattern of life as millions live it and as it may be lived by millions more if the past half-century's trend towards greater material well-being is not reversed.

In looking towards the future it is sometimes

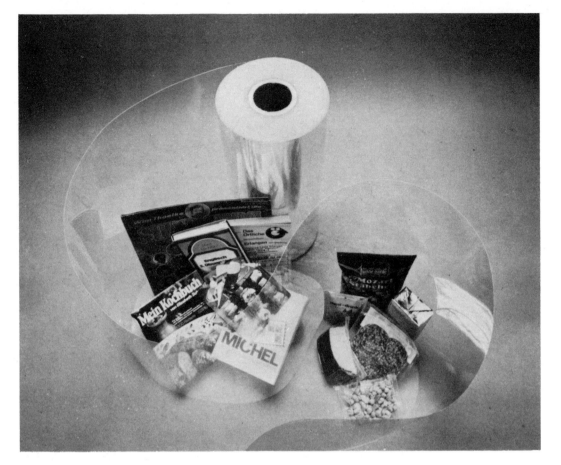

illuminating to reflect on the past. Unilever was not founded in easy circumstances, and Unilever's half-century has been economically one of the most turbulent and politically one of the most violent in history. At the same time there has been a widening prospect of well-being for mankind at large, if only the violence can be contained. Amid the tumult Unilever has demonstrated a determination to survive—and prosper—and a willingness to adapt in order to do so: qualities which have enabled it to contribute to a rising standard of living in the past and show every sign of continuing to enable it to do so in the future.

Longevity is of the essence of corporations and Unilever has the stuff of longevity in it. The East India Companies of England and the Netherlands lasted a couple of centuries. There seems to be no reason, barring universal catastrophe, why Unilever, given competent management, should not last as long or a good deal longer.

Above: Polypropylene products—'4P', Germany.

Opposite: The present headquarters of Unilever NV, Museumpark, Rotterdam.

Pages 142 and 143: The headquarters of Unilever Ltd, Blackfriars, London, is under renovation. This is an artist's impression of how it will look when it is completed. The appearance will then be closer to the original design approved by the first Lord Leverhulme before his death in 1925.

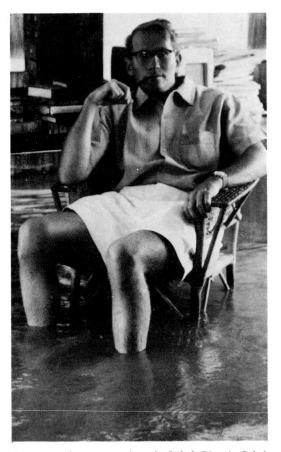

*In 1959 a planter voyaged up the Labuk River in Sabah
and started to establish a new oil palm plantation in
uninhabited jungle. Today it has its own oil mill,
village—even golf course—and over 2,000 people live
there. This was not accomplished without contention
with the vicissitudes of nature. This planter (not the
original one) typifies the phlegm needed to overcome
nature and build a business!*

Index

Advertising, 69, 74, 81
    factory foods, 64
    margarine, 29
    soap, 32, 58
Africa, 26, 53, 81–89, 91
African & Eastern Trade Corporation, 5
Allied Breweries, 79
America, Central, 130
Animal feeds, 20, 65
    per cent of total turnover (1946), 60
    per cent of total turnover (1977), 88
Asia, 44, 116
Austria, 44

Batchelors Foods Ltd, 52, 62
Belgium, 64
Birds Eye Foods Ltd, 52, 64, 99
Birdseye, Clarence, 36
Board, 22, 23, 52, 106–109
Brand names, 45, 69, 109
Brazil, 130
Butter, 20
    protection, 26–27, 41–44

Canada, 92, 93, 95
Canned food, 52, 60, 61
Centralisation, 104–5
Chemicals, 81
    see also Petro-chemicals
China, 44

Common Agricultural Policy, 92
Commercial Plastics, 79
Continent
    see Europe
Continental Committee, 22
Convenience foods, 36, 52, 56, 61–68
Cooper, Sir Francis D'Arcy (1882–1941), 6,
    10, 23, 29
Czechoslovakia, 44

De-centralisation, 104–105, 110
Dehydration, 62
Detergents, 52, 56, 60, 106, 117
    per cent of total turnover (1946), 60
    per cent of total turnover (1977), 88
    Product Co-ordinator, 105–106
    Tide, 93
    see also Soap
Dominions, 5
Ducas, Robert, 36

East India Companies, 140
Employees
    Unilever & subsidiaries (1978), 117
Equalisation Agreement, 9
Europe, 27, 41–44, 58, 91–92
European Economic Community, 55, 91–93
Fats
    see Oils and fats

Foods, 5
  canned, 52, 60, 61
  convenience, 36, 52, 56, 61–68
  factory, 64
  frozen, 52, 62–68, 106
  see also under individual foods
'4P' Group, 74

Germany, 52
  frozen food, 64
  government intervention, 23, 41–44
  packaging, 74–75
  trade restrictions, 26
Ghana, 82, 117, 130
Ghee, 104
Government intervention, 23, 122–3, 130
Guinness, 82, 110

Hartogs, 2, 36
Harvard Advanced Management Programme,
  112
Hedley, Thomas, Ltd, 32
Heinekens, 56, 82, 110
Henkel, 26, 32
Heyworth, Geoffrey, 1st Baron Heyworth of
  Oxton, 25, 36, 52, 104
Hindustan Lever, 117
Hindustan Steel, 135
Holland
  see Netherlands
Holloway, E. R. Ltd, 79
Holpak Ltd, 79
Home Soap Executive, 22

I.G. Farben Industrie, 6
Imperial Chemical Industries, 6
India, 5, 104, 117, 130, 137
Indian Planning Commission, 135
Indian State Trading Corporation, 135
Iraq, 130
'Isation', 111

Japan, 117
Jurgens, 2, 23
Jurgens, Anton (1867–1945), 23

Klijnstra, G. D. A. (1912–1976), 130, 137

Latin America, 110
Lawry's Foods Inc, 95
Lever Brothers & Associates, 104
Lever Brothers Company, 32, 104
Lever Brothers Ghana Ltd, 117
Lever Brothers Ltd, 1, 5–6, 52, 74
  administration, 21–23
  soap & edible fats, sales, 45
Lever Brothers Nigeria Ltd, 117
Lever, William Hesketh, 1st Viscount
  Leverhulme of the Western Isles (1851–
  1925), 2, 5, 6, 36, 69
  will, 116
Leverhulme Trust, 115–116, 118
Liptons, 95
Luckman, Charles, 93

Mac Fisheries Ltd, 5
Management,
  structure, 21–22, 104–105, 110
  training and development, 111
Margarine, 1, 2, 5, 36
  advertising, 29
  future, 117
  health food, 88
  1930's, 19
  per cent of total turnover (1946), 60
  per cent of total turnover (1977), 88
  production rationalisation, 24
  trade restrictions, 26–27, 41, 92
  UK Margarine Executive, 22
Margarine Unie, NV, 24
Margarine Union, 1–2, 5, 6, 9, 74
Market Research, 74
Metal Box Ltd, 79
Middle East, 81
Monopolies Commission, 79–81

Nairn Williamson Ltd, 79
National Managements, 99, 104–106
National Starch, 95
Nationalisation, 130
Netherlands, 64
New York Stock Exchange, 19
New Zealand, 137
Niger Company, 5, 6
Nigeria, 5–6, 81, 82, 117
Nippon Lever Industries, 117
North America,
  Regional Management, 106
  see also Canada and United States of
  America

OECD, 55
Oils and fats, 1, 20, 24, 36
  Edible fats and dairy Co-ordinator, 106
  edible fats, sales, 45
  per cent of total turnover (1946), 60
  per cent of total turnover (1977), 88
Oils & Fats Executive, 22
Overseas Committee, 22, 106

Packaging, 64, 69, 74, 79
Palm Line, 82
Paper, 74
Pelling Stanley & Co, 5
Pepsodent Co, 52, 95
Petro-chemicals, 60
Plantations Group, 82
Plantations Lever au Zaire, 117
Plastics, 74–79
Pollution, 123
Printing, 74
Procter & Gamble, 32, 52, 93, 104, 106
Product Co-ordinators, 105–106
Product Development, 58, 99

Rijkens, Dr Paul (1889–1965), 10, 52, 104

Schicht, 2, 23, 44
Shipbuilding, 44
Shipping, 82
Sierra Leone, 82
Smith & Nephew, T. J. Ltd, 79
Soap, 1, 2, 5, 29, 32
  Lux, 32
  per cent of total turnover (1946), 60
  per cent of total turnover (1977), 88
  production rationalisation, 24–26
  sales, 36, 45
  Sunlight, 2, 60, 69
  see also Detergents
Special Committee, 21–22, 107–109

Tea, 95
Thames Board Mills, 74
Timber, 82
Transport, 74, 82
Turkey, 104, 117, 130

UAC International, 85–89, 106
  per cent of total turnover (1977), 88
  see also United Africa Company
Unilever
  administration, 21–23
  Board, 22, 23, 52, 106–109
  centralisation, 104–105
  decentralisation, 104–105, 110
  diversification, 60
  employees (1978), 117
  Equalisation agreement, 9
  growth, 117
  Home Soap Executive, 22
  management, 21–23, 104–112
  National Managements, 99, 104–106
  Oils and Fats Executive, 22
  Overseas Committee, 22, 106
  Product Co-ordinators, 105–106
  Regional Management, North America, 106
  sales, soap & fats, 45
  sales, total value (1978), 116
  Special Committee, 21–22, 107–109
  turnover (1946), 60
  turnover (1977), 88
  UK Margarine Executive, 22
  world ranking, 139
Unilever-Emery, 110
Unilever Ltd, 9
  profits, 23
  shareholders, 115–116
  soaps & edible fats, sales, 45
Unilever NV, 9, 44
  profits, 23
  shareholders, 115–116
  soaps & edible fats, sales, 45
United Africa Company (UAC), 5, 22, 36, 81–85, 91
  per cent of total turnover (1946), 60
  rationalisation, 26
  shareholders, 117
  see also UAC International
United Kingdom
  foods 45, 52, 62, 64
United States, 93–99
  anti-trust, 130
  detergents, 52
  product development, 58
  trade protection, 27

Van den Berghs, 2, 9, 21, 23, 52
Vanaspati, 104

Wall's, T. & Sons Ltd, 5, 99
Watson, Angus & Co Ltd, 5
Wilson, Professor C. H., 137

Woodroofe, Sir Ernest, 113

Zaïre, 117